But Who Do You Say That I Am?

Raphael M. Obotama

authorHOUSE®

AuthorHouse™
1663 Liberty Drive
Bloomington, IN 47403
www.authorhouse.com
Phone: 1 (800) 839-8640

Published by AuthorHouse 04/08/2016

ISBN: 978-1-5049-8694-6 (sc)
ISBN: 978-1-5049-8693-9 (e)

Library of Congress Control Number: 2016904770

Print information available on the last page.

Contents

Acknowledgement

As this book has finally become a reality, I have every reason to be grateful to a lot of people who in one way or the other had been of immense help to me. The success story of this book cannot be complete without the help they rendered directly or indirectly. First I am thankful to God for the inspiration. I am grateful to His Excellency the Most Rev. David Kagan, the Bishop of Bismarck diocese who in spite of his busy schedule took some time out to thoroughly read through the manuscript. My thanks go also to Fr. Paul Becker, the Pastor of Corpus Christi Parish, Bismarck who not only read through the manuscript but accepted to write a foreword for this book. My Co-associate, Fr. Terry Wipf who is always ready to swap schedules with me whenever I need some time to clear some pressing work.

My appreciation also goes to the members of Staff here in Corpus Christi Church. We are more of a family than workplace colleagues, a family where everybody is ready to help out whenever anybody is in need of any assistance. I attribute this also to the dynamic leadership of the Pastor, Fr. Paul. I appreciate you all, Tracy Kraft, Loretta Arntz, Cindy Anderst, Jennifer Braun, Mariah Conner, Mary Janusz, Sr. Ivo Schoch, Jane Bosch, Niel Heinze, Bridget Johnson and Colleen Reinhardt.

Finally I appreciate the good relationship I enjoy with the people of God here in Corpus Christi Church. May we all continue to work together for the fulfilment of the kingdom of God here on earth.

Foreword

I am very pleased to offer a word of encouragement to the readers, as they access this document by Father Raphael Obotama. When I first met Father Raphael, he gifted me with a book about his father, a well-respected Catechist in the Catholic Church. I should have understood from that gift, how important the written word is to Father Raphael.

Across countries and cultures, in various times and places, the message of Jesus Christ has been a gift that enlivens the souls of believers. Father Raphael captures and presents that message, in a most succinct and effective manner.

Through his vast experiences, across countries and cultures, Father Raphael brings together a clear and concise presentation of the Gospel life and the activities and message of Jesus. Through this book, we learn of the world Jesus inhabited, the persons He encountered, the message He conveyed, and the impact of His life and teaching.

Father Raphael draws from his varied pastoral experiences in his native Nigeria and his adopted country of the United States, to compile a rich resource on Roman Catholic doctrines and beliefs, from which to address the "hungers" present in so many people's lives. The diversions and distractions that tempt so many away from the answers Jesus offers are clearly addressed in this challenging book. The "narrow road" that Jesus offered to His followers and to us, is the accomplished goal of this manuscript.

My compliments to Father Raphael, for his book, answering the question of Jesus, "But who do you say that I am?"

Reverend Paul Becker
Pastor, Church of Corpus Christi
Bismarck, North Dakota
2016

Introduction

He was born amid animals and died between two bandits. His thirty-three years on earth were shrouded in mystery, and He remains an enigma to many people. Who He is continues to confuse a lot of people even to this day, which leads to people interpreting Him from different points of view and from privileged positions.

More than two thousand years ago, a male child was born to a simple Jewish family. His birth was not in any way different from the ordinary Jew's of His time. Neither was His family any different. He grew up around His father's carpentry workshop, helping Him with the little chores He could as a young boy. He walked along the dusty alleys of their neighborhood, like any other young boy of His time. Apart from His parents, who were privy to the circumstance of His birth, no other person could have ever suspected that this child was anything out of the ordinary. At His presentation, which was required by tradition, two Old Testament individuals made startling statements regarding Him.

As He grew up, He started manifesting the powers in Him because it was time to start His mission. He went over to the widely known baptizer to be baptized by him. He then started His ministry thereafter. After the baptism, He started gathering men who would be His companions and carry on the work when His time had come to leave. He called them apostles. He started preaching about the kingdom of God, and the attention of the society was turned to Him. Many people followed Him, and His following turned into a movement, whose members later came to be known as Christians.

According to the *World Fact Book* of 2013, as cited by *Wikipedia*, 31.5 percent of the world's population identifies as Christian. They profess their faith in the Lord Jesus Christ. They read the Bible and follow the teachings of Jesus, the Son of God. This includes people of all ages, race, class and gender. The small group of initial followers whom Jesus gave the mandate to preach the gospel to all nations obeyed the command and carried it out well. In most countries of the world, there are churches that house different denominations of these believers. This religion, which has existed for about two thousand years, is still waxing stronger with many followers professing the faith.

At the onset of His ministry, Jesus asked a pertinent question, which is still very relevant today: "But who do you think I am?" This, of course, was a follow-up question He asked the apostles about who the people said He was. In my opinion, this seems to be the most important question in Christianity. A perfect answer to this question leads one to the Father. Answering this question correctly means one has truly known Christ, the Son of God. There is no way one can know the Father unless one knows the Son. When Jesus Christ put this question across to the apostles, only Peter was able to answer it correctly, and the Lord named him the leader of the apostles. Today the question is addressed to every person who professes to follow Jesus Christ. It is not a question that one should answer in a hurry because it tells a lot about one's personal relationship with the Master.

This book is based on the questions our Lord Jesus put forward to His apostles in the gospel: "Who do people say the Son of Man is?" which was then followed up with, "But who do you say that I am?" It is divided into two parts to accommodate the two questions. It is not a scholarly work in Christology. It is rather a reflection on some of the possible answers to the questions as they relate to us modern-day Christians.

The first part deals with the opening question: "Who do people say the Son of Man is?" Part 1 has five chapters.

In chapter 1, I reflect on the creation and how humanity lost their friendship with God. It treats the creation and fall of man, which led to the coming of the Savior. In chapter 2, I reflect on the fulfilment of the promise of God. God had promised to send a redeemer, and at the appointed time, He sent His Son. In chapter 3, I discuss the difficulties that the people were thrown into as a result as they struggled to identify Christ. The appearance of the Son of God on earth brought a lot of confusion as people had varied opinions of Him, and they kept asking Him who He was. Chapter 4 reflects on the different divine testimonies pointing to Jesus as the Messiah. The Father Himself had to personally introduce Him to the people at His baptism, and there were other divine pronouncements through the holy men and women of the time. Even with some divine testimonies about Him, it was still difficult for people to know Him. Chapter 5 reflects on His question to the apostles, which was prompted by the different opinions of people about Him. He asked them, "Who do people say the Son of Man is?" When He put the question to the apostles, they told Him what they heard people said about Him, which of course did not represent who He was. He went on further to ask them a follow-up question, which forms part 2 of this book.

Part 2, which actually deals with the title question of this book, "But who do you say that I am?" not only reflects on the event of that moment but also turns the question to individual Christians in the modern times. This part has six chapters. I begin this part with the question: why this question? Here I reflect on how many people have different opinions based on their own understanding. This is followed by a chapter I dedicate to those I refer to as dual-persona Christians. This chapter treats those who wear the masks of Christians but live like nonbelievers, people whom the Lord refers to as honoring Him with their lips while their hearts are far away from Him. Next, I ask the reader to make the question personal. Chapter 10 reflects on the answer that Peter gave to the Master: "You are the Christ." Once someone answers this question this way, it becomes a commitment. This means you know and recognize Him as the Lord. Then you are ready to follow His way of life and do what He asks you to do. The last chapter deals with people who come to know Christ through their personal encounter with Him. Most of the people who publicly confessed Him were personally touched by Him, like the woman at the well, who initially questioned Christ why He as a Jew should demand water from a Samaritan. She said, "I can see that you are a prophet," and ran back to the village to personally invite the villagers to come see a prophet.

There are some followers of Christ today, just like in the days of Christ, who play a double role. So the question that Christ asked could also be a way of saying, "Do you think I'm someone to be toyed with?" He also knew that some are following Him with ulterior motives. The question was to challenge their sincerity. Are all the people who profess to follow Him truly genuine? That was why He said that some were just honoring Him with their lips while their hearts were far away from Him. Who are these people?

To know how one is related to Jesus, one needs to make the question personal. Try to answer the question as if it is addressed directly to you. "Who do I say Jesus is?" The answer one gives to this question helps one to know one's relationship with the Master. Answering like Peter, "You are the Christ," is not just a verbal utterance but a commitment to the course of Christ. This book helps one to reflect on the big question of Jesus Christ. In this culture, a lot of people say something with their lips, but in their heart of hearts, they believe something else. It is good for followers of Christ to search their hearts and minds and come face-to-face with their faith in Jesus.

A lot of those who had personal encounters with Jesus came to believe and openly proclaimed Him. Martha said "Yes Lord, I believe that you are the Messiah, the Son of God…" John 11:27. The idea of this book is to lead us to question our relationship with Christ after several years of encounter with Him. Can we sincerely reecho the statement of Martha, and if so, do we act that out in our relationship with one another? If the answer is in the affirmative, then we can say truly that we have the right answer to the question "But who do say that I am?"

After reading through the book, I would expect the reader to reflect and try some personal answers to the question, which is as old as Christianity and yet not given so much attention by its adherents. In your heart, can you as a Christian personally and sincerely answer this question, "But who do you say that I am?"

Part 1

Who Do People Say the Son of Man Is?

1

In the Beginning

It is human nature to ask questions, Who? What? When? Where? Why? How? History as a source of knowledge is based on this set of inquiries. A good knowledge of the past prepares the present for the future. That is why storytelling is a fundamental feature in human developmental culture. In some cultures, oral tradition is essential in handing down history and the preservation of heritage. The biblical culture takes a cue from this. The story of the beginning of things is seen in the opening statement of the book of the Holy Scripture: "In the beginning, God created the heavens and the earth" (Genesis 1:1).

St. John, in the first chapter of his gospel, records, "In the beginning was the Word and the Word was with God and the Word was God" (John 1:1). According to his record of this great beginning, everything was made through this *Word*. "All things were made by Him; and without him was not anything made that was made" (John 1:3). St. Paul confirms this assertion in his letter to the Colossians: "For by Him all things were created, both in the heavens and on earth, visible and invisible, whether thrones and dominion or rulers or authorities, all things have been created through Him and for Him" (1 Colossians 1:16). The creative energy by which every creature under the heavens got its life is identified here as "the Word."

To address any lingering doubt regarding who this Word might have been, St. John goes on to clearly identify Him by saying, "The Word became flesh and dwelt among us" (John 1:14). By this statement, he shows that he is referring to Christ, the Son of the Living God, who came to live among us. This Word existed from the beginning of time. He is the source of everything that was made, and at the appointed time, He came down to live with them in flesh and blood. He that was from the beginning, who is now and will remain forever, took up flesh and walked the dusty roads of His Jewish neighborhood just like any ordinary Jew of His time. This is a deep mystery.

John, in these opening verses, writes to show the active role of the second person of the Trinity in the creation history. Here John presents Jesus as the "He" who was there from the beginning of time. In John's narrative, before the ages began, Jesus had a clear identity with the Father, and when He became man, he identified with us humans.

In the creation narrative, God saw that everything was good. At this point, the newly created world was only inhabited by animals, birds, and trees. One can only imagine how the world looked at that time without humans. God then said, "Let us make man in our own image." A stage was now set for the creation of man. The Bible tells us that "then the Lord God formed man of the dust of the ground, and breathed into his nostrils the breath of life, and man became a living being" (Genesis 2:7). Mere dust now puts on flesh by this divine act, and blood starts running through his veins, courtesy of the benevolent Creator. Man has life—he's breathing and moving about. He is now a living being, endowed with a brain so he can think, know, and decide in the face of good and evil which one to go for. Man is the only creature of God with that knowledge. The Catechism of the Catholic Church tells us that He created man to seek Him, to know Him, and to love with all his strength. God had a special affection for him, providing him with everything he stood in need of without asking. He looked up to God like a child resting on his mother's knees.

This good relationship that existed between God and man did not last long, for the devil destroyed it by luring man to disobey God. Man was not just given life but also the freedom to enjoy everything in the garden except for one thing: the tree of knowledge. Because this had been declared a no-go area, the devil used it as a target to confuse man and lure him to disobedience. In his usual sneaky ways, the devil went to the woman and asked if God had forbidden them from eating everything in the garden. The woman, in her innocence, not suspecting the intent of the devil, told him about the only tree that they were forbidden from eating from under the penalty of death. The woman was still obedient to God and had no reason to question the fidelity of God. When the devil is out to destroy, he applies every trick in his book. He countered what God had told them and assured her that they would not die. Here is what he told her: "For God knows that in any day you eat from it, your eyes will be opened, and you will be like God, knowing good and evil" (Genesis 2:3). As convincing as he was, the devil was able to deceive the woman into eating of the tree. "When the woman saw that the tree was good for food, and that it was delight to the eyes, and that the tree was desirable to make one wise, she took from its fruit and ate; and she gave also to her husband with her, and he ate" (Genesis 3:6).

In the opening sentence of his *Metaphysics*, Aristotle states that "all men by nature desire to know." The fall of man was instigated by the desire for knowledge. Tasting the fruit of knowledge of good and evil was what man saw as an easy way to possess knowledge and be like God. They embraced a new teaching propagated by a liar and a fraudulent creature—the devil. By this act, man chose to disobey God. At that moment, man said no to God's love and care because of his quest for knowledge. A new teaching, which the evil one used to stir up fantasy in the woman, was: "You will be like God, knowing good and evil" (Genesis 3:5). Man always wants to know, sometimes in a way that is not in agreement with the ways of God—a quest for knowledge that even now ignores the divine injunctions and challenges the traditional authority. This is a quest for knowledge that brings about a cultural revolution. Although Aristotle had said that man naturally desires to know, the source of knowledge is equally important. That is what contemporary minds seem to misunderstand.

Humanity lost out with the benevolent Creator, who had done everything to keep them happy. By this singular act of disobedience, man attracted a punishment on the earth and all that dwell therein.

Man had disobeyed God, but God took the initiative to restore him. He mapped out a plan for the salvation of man, promising to send a redeemer, one who was there from the beginning of time, His own begotten Son. He took part in the creation, knew man from the very beginning, and took it upon Himself to redeem man. He would be the Messiah who would set man free by taking up the human flesh in the form of man, undergoing suffering and death. The prophets spoke about this Messiah who would come to save the people of God. "Behold a virgin will be with child and bear a son, and shall call his name Immanuel" (Isaiah 7:14). *Immanuel* means "God is with us." The angel of the Lord who appeared to Joseph in a dream to tell him that the child Mary was carrying was from God also told him the mission of the child: "She will bear a son; and you shall call Him Jesus for He will save His people from their sins" (Matthew 1:21).

Man had distanced himself from God after the fall, but now God had chosen to come down and live among them in flesh and blood like them. The messianic prophet was emphatic on the mission of the Messiah, whom he said would deliver His people from their bondage. This, of course, was a pleasant piece of information for the people who erroneously had the feeling that the coming Messiah would surely liberate them from their subjection by the Roman authorities. Their expectations were for more of a political messiah than a spiritual one.

For many years, the people were waiting in hopes of beholding the Messiah. During this period of waiting, a lot of things happened. Sometimes they were alienated from God, and this led to their numerous exiles. For them, God had abandoned them, and they needed someone who would give them political freedom. The prophecy about the coming Messiah was welcome news for them.

2

And the Savior Came

It is in the nature of God to love and to forgive. He is good. In His divine goodness, God wants everyone to be saved; hence, in a mutual agreement with the Son, He sent Jesus to rescue fallen man. Here's what the Son said: "Therefore my Father loves me, because I lay down my life that I may take it up again. No one takes it from me, but I lay it down of myself. I have power to lay it down, and I have power to take it again. This command I have received from My Father" (John 10:17–18).

God consistently played His role as a loving Father right from the time of the fall of man so as to bring man back in union with Him. It is very interesting to note the caring attitude of God as portrayed after the fall. After Adam and Eve had eaten the fruit, they were ashamed and tried to hide from God, who had come down to look for them. Adam said, "I heard the sound of you in the garden, and I was afraid because I was naked; so I hid" (Genesis 3:10). After the initial reprimand by God, He cooled down His temper and continued being the caring and forgiving Father that He is. The scripture tells us His next move. "The Lord God made garments of skin for Adam and his wife" (Genesis 3:21).

The Catechism of the Catholic Church states, "After his fall, man was not abandoned by God. On the contrary, God calls him and in a mysterious way, heralds the coming victory over evil and his restoration from his fall" (CCC410). In the Old Testament, He made a covenant with Abraham that his descendants would be many and that he shall be the father of the nations. He used some important Old Testament figures to play the redemptive act until the appointed time. During this transitory period, God reached out to the people through some Old Testament figures. Moses played the minister who led the people out from slavery to freedom. He was a prefiguration of Christ the redeemer. In his dealings with the people, he kept reminding them of the plan of God for them. On one occasion, he told them, "The Lord your God will raise up for you a prophet like me from among you, from your countrymen, you shall listen to him" (Deuteronomy 18:15).

According to this divine arrangement, he led the people out of Egypt through the Red Sea, which is a prefiguration of the new people of God—the Christians walking through the water of baptism to the Promised Land. God fed the people of Israel in the desert with manna from heaven. Jesus was a witness to this as He later told the Jews, who were bragging about how they were fed in the wilderness. He told them who gave them the food. "It was not Moses who gave you bread it is my Father who gives you the true bread" (John 6:32). The Father, who gave their fathers the food to support their strength, was now giving them a spiritual bread in Him. The journey of the chosen people through the water of the Red Sea and the desert prefigure the pilgrimage of the new people of God.

The prophets of the old dispensation also spoke about the redemption of man through a Messiah. Isaiah, the messianic prophet, kept prophesying about the messianic era when there would be peace and tranquility. All through the Old Testament, we see God always playing the role of a caring God who remains faithful to His covenant even in the face of the infidelity of the people.

The Redemption

"But when the fullness of time had come, God sent forth his son" (Galatians 4:4).

The death of Christ was not an accident. It was prearranged by the Father, and the Son, Jesus Christ, totally subscribed to it, but this of course was to be manifested in time. St. Paul says, "But when the fullness of time had come," meaning "at the appointed time." This places our salvation as one divine plan in the history of man. God had elected a time for this to happen; it could not have been otherwise. The salvation of the world was a timed program. God works strictly according to time. Matthew describes the historic moment when the "time had come." It was in the garden of Gethsemane. Here Jesus addressed his sleeping apostles. "Are you still sleeping and resting? Look, the hour has come and the Son of man is to be delivered into the hand of sinners" (Matthew 26:45). Before now, he had told his blessed mother at the wedding feast in Canna: "Woman what concern is that to you and me? My hour has not yet come" (John 2:4)—the hour of deliverance, the hour of salvation.

The fall of man was not in the divine plan, but it instigated the salvation, according to the divine mercy. Man fell, and the divine mercy was hovering around, waiting for the time appointed by God to salvage humanity. He had already set a timetable for the redemption of man. Every event leading to the salvation of man was strictly according to plan. The events portrayed God's attributes of justice and mercy. In the preface of the immediate old translation of Mass, we used to say, "In love you created man, in justice you condemned him but in mercy you redeemed him." Man has been in the plan of God's mercy ever since creation. It is obvious that if God had not wanted to save man, He would have given him up to eternal damnation. One known fact about God is that He works according to His own time and we humans are supposed to go by that. His will must always prevail.

The second part of the statement is "God sent forth His son." This means the initiative was of God. The response of Christ is equally important here. God did not force Him. He agreed to do it. In a statement in the gospel, He says, "Greater love has no one than this that one lay down his life for his friends" (John 15:13). The one through whom everything was made lays down His life for the creatures He now refers to as friends, no creator-creature relationship but pals. What a privilege! This can only be done by one who is extremely humble. St. Paul talks about this when he says, "And being found in human form, He humbled Himself, becoming obedient unto death, even death on a cross" (Philippians 2:8). He gave up His own freedom and will for the sake of our redemption. In the garden of Gethsemane, during His passion, after praying that His father should take away the bitter cup from Him, the Lord Jesus immediately threw Himself into the will of His father by saying "not according to my will but thy will be done" (Luke 22:42). The will of God is always to be adhered to in everything, even at our own discomfort. This action challenges us, His "friends," who sometimes run away from the will of God to seek our own comfort. Sometimes we try to force our will on God.

To show that the hour is indeed here, St. Luke records what happened when Jesus went on one occasion into the synagogue. The passage from the book of the prophet Isaiah that was presented to Him when He entered the synagogue spelled out the mission of the suffering servant. "The spirit of the Lord is upon me; He has sent me to bring glad tidings to the lowly, to heal the broken hearted, to proclaim liberty to the captives and release to the prisoners, to announce a year of favor from the Lord and a day of vindication by our God, to comfort all who mourn" (Isaiah 61:1). After He had finished reading the passage, the people were just looking at Him. They must have been pondering some questions in their minds as to who this person was. He told them in Luke 4:21 that the awaited time had finally arrived. He hereby presented Himself to them as the fulfilment of that prophesy.

After the first man and woman disobeyed God, they and the generations after them were like prisoners, groping in the darkness of their sins. As they waited for their redemption, they relied on the utterances of the prophets. The anointed Messiah was to come from the tribe of David. The prophet had foretold of this fact. "But as for you Bethlehem Ephrata, Too little to be among the clans of Judah, from you One will go forth for Me to be ruler in Israel. His goings forth are from long ago from the days of eternity" (Micah 5:2). The deliverance from their sins was the primary reason of the coming of the son of man. St. Paul says, "We have all sinned and fall short of the glory of God." He came to restore humanity once again to God, to the glory man had from the beginning of time. In the salvation arrangement, therefore, there would be the retribution by way of atonement, a sacrifice that would pacify the Father. The sacrificial lamb was none other than the only son of the Father—the Word that was in the beginning with God, a Word that would become flesh and dwell among us. He would have to pay the supreme price so as to fulfill what was prearranged from "the days of eternity."

The fallen humanity had waited in hope for the fulfilment of the promise of God to His people to send a messiah as the prophets had spoken about Him many years before. When He eventually arrived, there was an ocean of confusion as to who He really was. The messiah they were expecting would not come in the manner they saw Him. He was one among them. For most of them, He could not have been the messiah, because they knew

His parents and siblings. They could not accept the idea of a God among them in human flesh. They said among themselves, "Is not this the carpenter's son? Is not his mother called Mary, and his brothers, James and Joseph and Simon and Judas?" (Matthew 13:55). Their problem was that He arrived in a manner they did not expect. "But we know where this man is from; when the messiah comes, he will simply appear, no one will know where he comes from" (John 7:17). Those in this school of thought continued to sow seeds of doubt in the minds of the people, which brought confusion. Some of them had the courage to openly question Him about who He really was, if He was the Christ. "The Jews gathered around Him, and were saying to Him, 'How long will you keep us in suspense? If you are the Christ tell us plainly'" (John 10:24). For many people of His time, His presence evoked some curiosity.

Curiosity is a natural phenomenon, which sometimes pushes people to speculate when the right answer is not readily available. In most cases, it gives room for rumors, which can lead to false information and erroneous suppositions. Hypotheses are developed to explain some strange phenomena. Most of these are seen in mysteries of which religion is paramount. Sometimes the answers are difficult to come by. Some people fall back to the realm of faith to solve their mysteries, while others go ahead to confront it. The case of Jesus raised a series of questions in people's minds and still does even after so many years of Christianity. The puzzles still remain widely unsolved. As the Jews of His time were asking Him, many people today, even Christians, are still asking the identity of Christ, some in words, but many in actions.

3

Who Are You?

When a person is asked, "Who are you?" it could mean one of the following: either the questioner genuinely wants to know about the individual, which may mean he or she is interested in the individual, or the questioner has some reservations about him or her, which may be a result of some lingering doubt, and needs some clarification. It carries much weight if the doubt is caused by some suspected activities of the individual. Such a person would be subjected to an increasingly severe scrutiny by the inquirer.

Doubt is a very powerful feeling. It could be strong enough to erode the faith of even the most strong and faithful Christian. The *Oxford Dictionary* defines it as "A feeling of uncertainty or lack of conviction." Doubt gives room for questions. Once a person is in doubt, he or she asks a lot of questions and needs a lot of proof to dissipate the doubt. As humans and especially as Christians, many of us are faced with doubts often, as there are many things that we do not understand because of our limited knowledge and sometimes limited or conflicting information. In the middle of doubts, people sometimes directly ask God for proof or signs so as to satisfy their curiosity. In the Old Testament times, some people dared to question God. Moses even asked God His name when he was asked to go on a mission for God. "Behold I am going to the sons of Israel, and I will say to them, 'The God of your fathers has sent me to you.' Now they may say to me, 'what is his name?' what shall I tell them?" (Exodus 3:13). Thomas was among the apostles and had been with Christ for a long time, but when he was presented with the story of the resurrection and appearance of their master in his absence, he did not buy it. He doubted it so much that he told his colleagues, "Unless I see in His hands the imprint of the nails, and put my finger into the place of the nails, and put my hand into his side, I will not believe" (John 20:25).

Doubt is not unbelief, but some doubts do certainly lead to unbelief. Some doubts just need a little clarification, as in the case of the innocent doubt of the Blessed Virgin Mary at the annunciation when she asked the angel Gabriel, "How can this happen since I do not know man?" Thomas's case was a very strong doubt that turned into unbelief. As he put it, "Unless I see the nail marks and put my finger in the nail mark, I will not believe." When Jesus appeared again after seven days and asked him to perform his *experiment*, as he said he would before believing, Christ told him, "Don't be unbelieving but believe." Sometimes people's doubts are so strong that they are just not ready to accept any answer. This is when faith is in danger. Sometimes if the object of doubt is a living person, they are ready to confront him or her with some questions for clarification. Doubts have the power to retard progress. In religion, doubt is a very serious ailment that can threaten one's faith. When people are in doubt, they start questioning everything in the church and sometimes question the authenticity of the church teaching.

Throughout His lifetime, people kept challenging Jesus Christ because of His ministerial style; He did not teach like other rabbis. He taught with authority. A lot of His teachings became a thorn in the flesh of religious leaders. Some of them asked Him for signs to prove His identity, though He had performed miracles before them. It was quite difficult for some of them to believe in Jesus, given the nature of His appearance on the religious terrain. "What then do you do for a sign, so that we may see, and believe you?" (John 6:30). In spite of all the signs and wonders He had performed among them, they were still doubtful because their minds and hearts were closed against Him. They were biased. It is difficult for people who are biased to believe or trust. If one thinks that those days were over, such a person should better have a rethink because today modern Christians are still operating under this show-me-a-sign attitude. So many Christians today are still looking for signs—miracles. That is the reason the evil one is very active, trying to show his own signs and gain adherents to himself. The gullible ones follow. Whoever accepts a miracle as the only sign to believe in God is not a true believer. He or she is sure to fall, for God's miracles are revealed to believers not doubters looking for something to hold on to. In today's world, people want to understand before they believe. The inspirational words of St. Augustine can very well fit in here: "Understanding is the reward of faith. Therefore, seek not to understand that you may believe, but believe that you may understand."

Some people ask questions when they do not understand something or when they do not recognize the signs that are presented before them. That was the same scenario that played out during the time of Christ. Many a time, the signs were very glaring, yet these people failed to see or understand. In the gospel, for example, when Jesus warned His apostles to beware of the leaven of the

Pharisees and that of Herod, not understanding what He meant, they thought that He was referring to the fact that they had no bread, which made Jesus query them thus,

> "When I broke the five loaves for the five thousand, how many baskets full of fragments did you take up?" they said to him "twelve." "Also when I broke the seven loaves to the four thousand how many large baskets full of fragments did you pick up?" And they said seven. And he said to them, "How is it that you do not understand?" (Mark 8:19–21)

Probably the disciples were just taking the multiplication of the loaves as a normal cause of events. They failed to see the divine hand in the miracle of the multiplication of the loaves. The people of the time of Jesus, like these apostles, saw the signs but could not interpret them. Sometimes Christians take some of the signs before them as normal; they do not see the hand of God in the events of their lives.

Signs and wonders of the power of God abound around us, yet we keep asking questions concerning our future. When John sent his disciples to question Jesus if He was the messiah, He simply asked the disciples to go and tell John the signs that had taken place among the people, which matched with the messianic prophesy. "Go and report to John what you have seen and heard: the blind receive their sights, the lame walk, lepers are cleansed, and the deaf hear, the dead are raised up and the poor have good news preached to them" (Luke 7:22). These were signs of the fulfillment of the prophecies of Isaiah that would be associated with the messiah. The prophet had outlined signs of the messianic times. "Then will the eyes of the blind be opened and the ears of the deaf be unstopped" (Isaiah 35:5).

In John 8:25, the authorities, apparently confused by His utterances, had put this question directly to Jesus: "Who are you?" His answer to them was that He is the "He," meaning the one they were waiting for. Hear him: "When you lift up the son of man, then you will realize that I am He" (John 8:28). This resonates with the answer that God gave to Moses from the burning bush: "Tell the Israelites, 'I am has sent me to you'" (Exodus 3:14).

In one of their many confrontations with Jesus, the Jews asked Him for a sign as cited above. His response to them was: "I told you and you do not believe me. The works that I do in my Father's name, these testify to me" (John 10:25). At the level they were operating, He knew that no amount of miracles would have convinced them because their hearts were already closed toward Him.

During his triumphal entry into Jerusalem, Matthew tells us "the whole city was shaken and asked, 'Who is this?' and the crowds replied, 'This is Jesus the prophet, from Galilee" (Matthew 21:3). Many people had already known Him as a prophet while quite a lot did not.

At His trial before Pilate, the prosecutors presented Jesus as a criminal, but when He gave His own testimony, telling Pilate that He came to bear witness to the truth, Pilate was left confused. "'My kingdom is not of this world,' he said, 'Otherwise my father would have sent a legion of angels to fight for me.' 'Are you a king then?' the puzzled Pilate asked Him" (John 18:36–37). It was at this scene that Jesus introduced a new word to Pilate— *truth*, a word which Jesus said He came to bear witness to. Pilate was eager to know more about truth. He was probably used to the colloquial use of the word; this very use by Jesus in His trial introduced a new angle to truth as an embodiment of the divine. The true God, as seen in His son standing before them, was still yet unrevealed to them.

On the cross, only one of the thieves (though I'm not sure he did know him personally) testified that he was an innocent man. He could recognize some attribute of a good person in Him. He may not have had any opportunity of witnessing Christ's miracles, but he could tell that this man was certainly not like them on that cross. There must have been something revealed to him about Jesus. I guess the words of Jesus to Peter could also go for this man here, for it was not flesh and blood that had revealed it to him. The robber went ahead and seized that golden opportunity of his being so close to the divine for the first time to present his final prayer request to Christ, his last favor from the man he knows has the key to his eternal joy. "Jesus, remember me when you come into your kingdom" (Luke 23:42). It is interesting to note that he even knew Christ as a king. He just spent a few hours with Jesus and was able to know Him just like the woman at the well. He was not disappointed because Christ promised him a life in paradise that same day. He achieved what some people who had spent a longer time with Christ could not because of their unbelief. By the special grace of God, a sinner can become a saint in an instant.

Sometimes salvation comes at the stroke of one's end of life. These are, of course, rare opportunities. One should therefore not wait for the last-minute rush through the gate of the kingdom. I had the opportunity to baptize a condemned armed robber at the stake in 1989 before he was publicly executed in Nigeria. I was invited by the city authority to pray for him before his execution, and when I approached him to pray for him, he asked me if there was anything I could do so that God would receive his soul. Upon inquiry, he told me he was not baptized. I asked him if he would like to be baptized, and he responded in the positive. The only water available at that moment was the Holy Water I had brought along with me. So I went ahead and baptized him there at the stake. I know there would be some debate about this and some people may even say he had no other option, but in my ministry to these kinds of people, I have asked another condemned robber like him before if he would want me to pray for him and he refused even to be prayed for before execution. He told me that he did not want my presence. It is my belief that the armed robber went to heaven because he actually asked for the baptism of his own volition. Now that was quite a digression from the main discussion here.

The days after the crucifixion and death of our Lord Jesus were the darkest and most traumatic for the apostles who had been with Christ for a period of time. In this moment of confusion and anxiety, there was the announcement that the Lord had risen from the dead, but some of them could not fathom it. It sounded too strange for some of them to believe, while some were struggling to understand. The disciples on the way to Emmaus in a bid to explain the Easter events to a "stranger" who had just joined them on the way as they were traveling along displayed some level of doubt on the resurrection story. The stranger happened to be Jesus Himself. Hear them:

> But we were hoping that he would be the one to redeem Israel; and besides all this, it is now the third day since this thing took place. Some women from our group, however, have astounded us; they were at the tomb early in the morning and did not find his body; they came back and reported that they had indeed seen a vision of angels who announced that he was alive. (Luke 24:21–23)

That was nothing short of a statement of doubt. They did not understand the resurrection, which was some sort of a new and strange thing to them. That was what prompted the doubt. They could not understand how a person who had been in the tomb for three days could come back to life. The stranger had to repudiate them by calling them foolish for failing to understand all that was written in the scriptures about Him. Does this mean that they doubted the Master's words to them that He would rise in three days? I think it's more of a lack of understanding of the Master. Hear what he said to them: "Oh how foolish you are, How slow of heart to believe all that the prophets spoke! Was it not necessary that the messiah should suffer these things and enter his glory?" (Luke 24:25–27). In spite of this, they were still doubtful until they broke the bread with the risen Lord later that evening in their house.

Another occasion in which doubt played a significant challenge to the struggling faith of the apostles was on the sea when the Lord appeared to them walking on the water. Peter and probably the rest of the apostles doubted it was their Master. Peter spoke up. "Lord, if it is You, command me to come to You over the water" (Matthew 14:28). The other apostles in the boat, who were equally afraid, were probably watching to see what would happen to Peter so as to know what to do next. The circumstance that Peter was faced with was such that he could probably not think right. He was physically on the sea and at the same time spiritually thrown into a sea of doubt. He had to be very sure that it was truly the Master before he could make any move—hence the request to the Master: "If it is you, call me." Even after the assurance by the Master, he lost his courage as he was walking on the sea. That was when he started to sink. He lost his faith because he lost his focus on Jesus and focused on the sea around him. Once a follower of Christ loses his or her gaze on Jesus and focuses on the turbulence around him or her, the person loses his or her balance. That is what leads to the weakening of one's faith and the outcome is lots of questions and loss of faith in God's power to save.

Asking a person, "Who are you?" could be an indication of not recognizing the authority of the individual. In contemporary Christianity, we inadvertently ask this question when we challenge the authority of the church. Sometimes we question the teachings of the church. In contemporary society, some of the teachings of the church are no longer very popular within a certain generational bracket of churchgoers, such as the church's teachings against abortion, contraception, gay marriage, and so on. Challenging such teachings is directly challenging God because Christ said, "The one who listens to you listens to me, and the one who rejects you rejects me and he who rejects me rejects the one who sent me" (Luke 10:16). So as long as the church maintains her stand on the issues above, any member of the church who challenges that sets him- or herself against whom the church receives her teaching authority from.

To be in a proper relationship with Jesus, doubts should not be entertained. This could lead to loss of faith and eventually unbelief. Let us remind ourselves once again what Jesus told Thomas: "Do not be unbelieving but believe" (John 20:27).

In this age of Internet and social media, so many people within the younger generation prefer to get their instructions from the Internet. Most of the teachings on the Internet do not agree with the teachings of the church. Such teachings can bring confusion in the minds of the young ones who maintain the largest demographic in the Internet community.

4

The Divine Testimony

In the annals of human existence, great people and very important events form the bedrock of history. Calendars are mostly dated according to these events and personalities. Every great person in history is known after he or she has lived on earth for a period of time, and his or her greatness is a result of his or her work. Historical events can only be recorded after they have taken place. No historical figure who ever walked the face of this earth was ever talked about prior to his or her birth. People only make it to the pages of history books after their achievements. There is only one person who made it to historical records before he was even born. According to Archbishop Fulton Sheen, writing about Christ in his book *The Life of Christ*, he referred to Him as the only person preannounced. This shows that His greatness existed even before He was born in the flesh. The chosen people were expecting His coming. Isaiah, the prophet, preannounced Him centuries before He came. "A virgin shall conceive and bear a son, and he shall be called Immanuel meaning God is with us" (Isaiah 7:14). When he eventually came into the world, there was a series of events and divine pronouncements that pointed to Him as the one who was to come.

The Announcements

At the verge of the fulfillment of the prophecies, the angel Gabriel was sent by God to Mary to announce the good news. Mary, a young innocent village girl, whose sole purpose in life was to please God, was understandably shaken at the sight of such a dreadful figure before her. She had never met an angel physically before in her life. In her simplicity, she never thought she was worthy to be visited by a messenger from heaven. The figure before her was, to say the least, a terrifying sight. The angel, who truly understood her fright, assured her that everything was okay. "Do not be afraid Mary, for you have found favor with God. Behold you will conceive in you womb and bear a son, and you shall name him Jesus" (Luke 1:30–31). Mary, who was still in a daze, managed to protest innocently before the angel that she had never known any man. When she was assured that the whole process would be through the power of the Holy Spirit, she willingly submitted to the will of God. She accepted to bring forth the Savior of the world.

Jesus Christ, the second person of the divine Trinity, though He existed from the beginning of time, was not known to humans until He took flesh in the womb of the Blessed Virgin Mary, which He did to fulfil the prophecy of Isaiah. It was necessary therefore that some chosen people be informed of the arrival of this Son of God.

As soon as He was born, the angels went to the shepherds who were tending their sheep in the field and announced to them the good news. The angel said to them, "Do not be afraid; for behold, I proclaim to you good news of great joy that will be for all the people. For today in the city of David a savior has been born for you who is messiah and Lord" (Luke 2:10–11). The long-expected messiah had finally arrived.

He was introduced as the "savior," which pointed to His messianic mission of saving His people from their sins, exactly as the angel told Joseph prior to the child's birth. The shepherds who were among those waiting for the redeemer of Israel received the news with excitement as they left their flock and went to see this child. They were the first set of humans who had the great privilege of being told who Christ really was—Messiah and Lord.

That was enough to convey the message of the fulfilment of God's promise to His people.

At His Presentation

When the days for purification were completed, the parents took this child to the temple in Jerusalem for the ritual presentation. As the couple entered the temple with the infant Jesus, they must have thought that they were the only people in the temple at that material time who knew the true identity of their child. It happened that two very important Old Testament figures were in the temple when they entered. Simeon, who had been told by God that he would not die until he had seen the Christ, took the child in his hands at the prompting of the Holy Spirit and blessed the Lord. This is how Luke reports the event: "He took him into his arms and blessed God, saying: 'Now, Master, you may let your servant go in peace, according to your word for my eyes have seen your salvation, which you prepared in the sight of all the people, a light for the revelation to the Gentiles, and the glory of your people Israel'" (Luke 2:28–32). After blessing the Lord, he made a very startling statement to the parents, "Behold this child is appointed for the fall and rise of many in Israel, a sign to be opposed" (Luke 2:34).

There was also a prophetess, who according to St. Luke was led by the Spirit to visit the temple at that moment, and she was blessed with the privilege of seeing this child. The two holy people here testified eloquently about this child to the amazement of even his parents. "But Mary treasured all these things, pondering them in her heart" (Luke 2:19)—a contemplative attitude one may say.

At His Baptism

Before Jesus appeared on the scene to be baptized, John the Baptist had spent quite a lengthy time talking to people and preparing them for the coming of Christ the Messiah. When Jesus approached him as he was giving the people the baptism of repentance, John the Baptist immediately recognized Him and pointed Him out to the world. "Behold the lamb of God who takes away the sin of the world" (John 1:29). He there and then became the first human to publicly introduce the Messiah to a "congregation."

Jesus the Messiah, whom John had spoken of as one "whose sandals" he was "not worthy to untie," surprisingly requested to be baptized by him. John was at first reluctant to baptize Him as he found himself not worthy, knowing who Christ was and probably thinking that his job was just to prepare the people for Him, not baptize Him about whom he had told the people: "He must increase and I must decrease." This was the man about whom he had said in reference, "I baptized you with water; but He will baptize you with the Holy Spirit" (Mark 1:8). This was a difficult one for him, but at the insistence of Jesus, however, John baptized him. He bore testimony to Him by showing Him to the world. He was doing what he was destined to do. "You go before the Lord to prepare his ways" (Luke 1:76).

John may have baptized people in their hundreds before this fateful day, and many people had witnessed him do that, but nothing in all that prepared them for what they were about to witness. At the moment of the baptism of Christ, there were many people at that site, but they did not fully grasp the mystery that was taking place—the baptism of the author of life. It was at the climax of this historic event that His Father made a very solemn confirmation of Him and formally presented Him to the world. Here is how Matthew records that supernatural phenomenon: "After Jesus was baptized, he came up from the water and behold, the heavens were open (for him), and he saw the Spirit of God descending like a dove (and) coming upon him. And a voice came from the heavens, saying, 'This is my beloved son, with whom I am well pleased" (Matthew 3:16–17). The people who were there probably heard the voice; it was the same voice that used to speak to their fathers from the mountain of God. Their fathers were used to hearing the voice of God from the clouds, but it was not of such magnitude, introducing His Son in flesh and blood to the people. Did the people really know what He was talking about? It seems this message was specifically meant for them since John the Baptist had already known Jesus. It is evident that this entire introduction did not register in the minds of the people, as later in His ministry they kept mistaking him for who he was not. This mistake grew along with Christ as He on several occasions had to personally tell the people who He was using different images as necessitated by the audience. At one point, He introduced himself as "the good shepherd" (John 10:11). At another, he was "the way the truth and the life" (John 14:6) and also "the living bread" (John 6:51). He used these images to drive home some lessons about Himself, which of course the people were very slow in understanding.

St John writes about Christ and says that He is very well known. "What was from the beginning, what we have heard, what we have seen with our eyes, what we have looked and touched with our hands concerning the word of life" (1 John 1:1). This in a way wraps up the whole salvation history.

"I Am"

When two people use an identical tag to introduce themselves, there is a great chance that they have a solid bond that ties them together; either by blood or special affinity, they are in some way identical. The first time we are presented with this phrase, "I AM," in the scriptures is in the burning bush experience of Moses when he was confronted by an unknown voice and he asked the voice from the burning bush to identify himself. The voice told him "I am who am." He even directed him to tell the people of Israel that "I Am" sent him. This was God himself talking to Moses. The Lord Jesus, who had told his disciples, "The Father and I are one," had no problem using it to identify Himself. Here is how John records it. "Jesus said to them, 'truly, truly I say to you, before Abraham was born I am'" (John 5:58). Going further he presents Jesus as saying to the people He was addressing, "When you lift up the Son of Man, then you will realize that I AM…" John 8:28. Here He drives home the point that John makes in his gospel that He was the Word that was with God from the beginning of time, who Himself was God.

All the above prophecies and statements of divine revelation were to show the people that He is the Christ who was to come into the world. He pointed out to the disciples on the way to Emmaus that all that had been written about Him in the law and the prophets had been fulfilled. They failed to understand all the signs that pointed to Him.

It can be very frustrating for a teacher who has spent quite a lot of time explaining something to students only to discover at the end that they did not get anything of what he or she had tried to teach them. From the prophets in the old covenant to Jesus Christ Himself in the new covenant, a lot has been said by way of introduction of the Messiah yet the people were very slow to understand. In spite of His presence among them in words and actions, they missed those and kept expecting the Messiah. One glaring example is the case of the disciples on the way to Emmaus on the resurrection Sunday who could not recognize their Master even as He explained the scriptures concerning Himself to them. If this could happen with those in His inner circle, what would the fate of the people outside His inner circle be?

In spite of all the divine revelations and prophetic preannouncements about this Messiah for the past two thousand years, the reality of His birth and His teachings, Christians have been battling with who Jesus really is as people keep coming up with different and confusing theories and even some conspiracies about Him. This has brought about many teachings that sometimes stem from individual understanding or how some individuals want to frame Jesus to suit their agenda. Books upon books have been published, some out rightly to mislead the people about the identity of Christ. Even those who profess to be Christians give varied interpretations of the life and teachings of Christ. As it was in the days of our Lord, which led Him to ask the question, the situation has not changed and the divine Master can still be heard asking, "Who do people say the son of Man is?"

The question that Jesus asked His disciples could also be interpreted to mean that He was trying to put them in a better perspective and arm them for the great ministry ahead of them. To let them know that people have varied opinions of Him. He knew ahead of time that the ministry would require a lot. The Catechism of the Catholic Church teaches us that God created man to know and to love him. We cannot love God unless we know and love His Son, Jesus Christ, whom He sent to save us. He came to show us the Father. With all these confusions and misrepresentations about Jesus Christ, it is therefore necessary for Jesus to keep on asking even now this pertinent question.

5

Who Do People Say the Son of Man Is?

He was in the world but the world did not know him, though the world was created through him. —John 1:10

In a culture where ratings determine the popularity of an individual or a group, people who put themselves out in the public arena do everything to maintain high ratings. Politicians watch out for polls and television networks put out programs that would put their ratings ahead of other competitors. Public office seekers running for elections are concerned with what people say and how they rate them. To a contemporary mind, this question may provoke such feelings—a search for ratings—but surely this question has nothing to do with public opinion or ratings.

In the history of great personalities of the world, Jesus Christ seems to be the most controversial figure. This is prompted by the misunderstanding of his personality, yet He remains one of the most written about and talked about in the history of humanity because even those who are not Christians still find it interesting to study Him. From the biological perspective, he was born of a woman betrothed to a man through the legally approved process in the Jewish sociocultural setup. Therefore, to an average Jew, there was no significant difference in his birth process that would have marked Him out as a very special person. He was like any other Jew of his time. As the people saw him, He had a father and a mother, like any regular Jewish boy. He started manifesting certain significant traits when He changed water into wine at a wedding feast in Canaan, Galilee, at the intercession of His Mother. Any human in any society in the world with the persona of Christ would be subject to speculations and opinions as people tried to attach some identity to Him. Sometimes myths are created around such figures to serve as some explanation for what people find difficult to fully interpret. In the time of Christ, people were confused about how to truly place this individual in order to define Him. Of course this went with a lot of erroneous concepts about Him. He appeared as a prophet and a healer. He was also a rabbi, though they recognized Him to have some extraordinary qualities. He did not teach like other rabbis; He taught with authority. Many people therefore had a different opinion of him. Certainly Jesus Himself was very much aware of this. He even knew that some of his disciples were equally confused about His true identity. He did not match the Messiah of their expectation.

In a situation where even His inner circle members could not fully understand Him, He needed to do something about it. He needed a dramatic way to drive the lesson into them. As is always the case, God does His things at the appointed time.

It happened in the region of Caesarea Philippi when, as usual, the Master was with His disciples, teaching them and telling them stories, and He put to them what might seem, in contemporary parlance, to be a premeditated, epoch-making question: "Who do people say the son of man is?" (Matthew 16:13). I call this premeditated because there was nothing within the scene of event at that material time that prompted the question. The question led to an inspirational answer by Peter, which the Master confirmed was revealed by the Father.

By "people" here, He was referring to the public, those outside His inner circle. It was clear that not everybody in the Jewish community was His disciple or belonged to His group. There were many who had no idea of His existence, while others just knew Him as a fellow Jew.

With this question, the Master was not really seeking a public opinion of Himself; He was using it as a teachable moment for the apostles who would soon be left alone physically on earth to continue the ministry. This was a lesson He had wanted them to learn—that not everybody would recognize his authority or understand their teaching.

Then, as it is today, people had diverse opinions of Him. Many outside His fold still have various opinions of Him. Step outside the Christian culture and listen to or read what people are saying about Him, especially in this age of technology. The Internet is agog with all sorts of doctrines, mostly erroneous, about the person of Jesus. There is so much about Him that Pope St. John Paul II titled one of his books on Christ *A Sign of Contradiction*. People saw Him and are still seeing Him from different prisms. Of course, He was meant to be like that. Remember the statement of Simeon at His presentation: "Behold this child is destined for the fall and rise of many in Israel" (Luke 2:34). So the question was, among other things, to put them on alert.

In response to the question, the apostles, who I believe did not grasp the significance of that question at that moment, put forward what they heard people said about their master. "Some say John the Baptist, others say Elijah; and still others, Jeremiah or one of the prophets"

(Matthew 16:14). They gave Him every other identity except His true identity. For the apostles, those were the correct answers to the question that He put forward to them. Those were truly the opinions of people outside the circle.

Is the opinion of non-Christians any different today? No. There are so many religious and secular institutions that view Jesus from some of these perspectives. Many other people view Jesus from their particular perspective. For the Muslims even today, He is still seen as a prophet, but they have nothing to do with Him.

Today, as it was then, I guess it would still be just as difficult to take Him at His word, given the number of charlatans parading the religious terrain as prophets, preachers, and healers. Who is who in this ocean of "spiritual leaders" or "men of God" is difficult to decipher. There is confusion today as much as there was in those days for those who are not properly catechized in authentic Christology. This, of course, goes to confirm what He had already said: that many would come in His name. "For many will come in my name, saying, 'I am Christ, and mislead many" (Matthew 24:5).

Did Jesus blame the public for not knowing His true identity? I am not sure the Master blamed them for not knowing Him at that level because He was kind of a "new thing" in their history—an enigma. He probably wanted it that way, remaining a mystery for a time; on many occasions, he had cautioned His disciples to tell no one about some revelation they happened to witness. A case in point here is the glory of the transfiguration, which He warned the privileged apostles not to mention to anyone until the Son of Man had risen from the dead. He probably wanted His true identity to be wrapped within the messianic secret until the appropriate time—after the resurrection. It is obvious that the Lord was not concerned with what the public said about Him. They still had a long time to learn about Him after He had gone. The question was probably another way of showing His disciples that the world did not know Him yet, which meant they had a lot of work to do in the area of evangelism.

There were many things they did not comprehend at that material time, which was one of the reasons He would send the Holy Spirit. He said the Holy Spirit would reveal to the people all that He had taught them. They needed a divine enlightenment to open their eyes to the divine actions being demonstrated among them by Jesus Christ.

The people who were used to seeing priests, prophets, and kings could not contemplate a God living among them in flesh and blood as they were. That was where they missed the point. The question here is, would the people have believed Him if He had descended from the sky in a parachute in their presence? That is left for conjecture.

From the time of His birth, Jesus Christ had been mostly misunderstood by the same people He came to save. His work among them was not seen as anything divine. Even when he performed miracles among them. They would read a different meaning into it. In the Gospel of Luke, when He cast out a mute demon and the person began to speak, they said, "He casts out demons by Beelzebub, the prince of demons" (Luke 11:15). His numerous encounters with the people always ended up in conflict. The people with whom He grew up would always say, "Is this not the carpenter's son?" Sometimes they even questioned His authority. At the scene of the healing of the paralytic in the Gospel of St. Mark, Jesus told the paralytic, "Child, your sins are forgiven." The people who witnessed the event, notably the religious authorities, said in their hearts, "Why does this man speak that way? He is blaspheming. Who but God alone can forgive sins?" (Mark 2:7). They questioned his authority to forgive sins. After the temple cleansing where he drove out the money changers, he was confronted by the chief priests, as Matthew records: "When he had come into the temple area, the chief priests and the elders of the people approached him as he was teaching and said, 'By whose authority are you doing these things? And who gave you this authority?'" (Matthew 21:23).

Even those closest to Him sometimes misinterpreted His actions. When he went to eat at the house of a Pharisee, the host, who had generously invited Him, had a shocking impression of Him when He saw Him interact with the sinful woman and said, "If this man were a prophet he would know who is touching him and what kind of woman she is. That she is a sinner" (Luke 7:39). He could not understand why Jesus would interact with a public sinner. This action, from their perspective, clearly showed them that He was not a prophet.

Within the thirty-three-year time frame He physically walked the face of the earth, His persona was as varied as the different people He came in contact with. In his book *A Generous Orthodoxy*, Brian McLaren has a chapter titled "The Seven Jesuses I Have Known." In this chapter, he explores Jesus as proclaimed by different faith and ideological traditions. Here are his varied models of Jesus: the Conservative Jesus, the Pentecostal/Charismatic Jesus, the Roman Catholic Jesus, the Eastern Orthodox Jesus, the Liberal Protestant Jesus, the Anabaptist Jesus, and the Jesus of the Oppressed. With each of these Jesuses, he presents the different notions of who people say the Son of Man is. When one looks at this chapter within the context of the prevailing question of Jesus under discussion in this book, one is bound to come out with the belief that even in contemporary Christianity, Jesus has various meanings to various people. This means He would get much the same answer to His question today as at that moment in Caesarea Philippi.

In this contemporary time, Jesus has been seen from different lenses. He is so much more often seen from personal or ideological perspectives than the objective perspective—the Savior whom the Father sent to redeem us. This sometimes poses a problem in evangelization. Each person or minister preaches the Jesus he or she knows, especially in some faith traditions that do not have a properly laid-down Christology. Non-Christians sometimes use this tool to criticize the Christian religion. I shall deal with this again in the follow-up question in part 2 of this book, as this seems to be a major problem that blocks Christian unity.

I'm just wondering what was in the minds of the apostles when the Master posed that question to them, wanting to know who people said He was. They could have exploited the situation to get to know more about their Master, but they did not. If He had not asked the follow-up question directed at the apostles, would they have dared to ask Him any further questions? Like who He really was? Did they even stop to ask themselves why the Master had asked them that question at that particular time? Or were they just thinking it was one of those casual questions the Master would ask just for the sake of conversation? If the later, they missed the depth of the question, which eventually turned out to produce for them a leader. This is a question that defines Christianity. Giving a proper answer to this question lays a good background for the Christian culture. Knowing what people think and how they view the Master forms a solid pedestal for a good and effective evangelism. The different shades of Christian doctrines that we have in our generation speak well about the different understandings of who the Son of Man is. If that question was again asked by Jesus today, the list of who people say the Son of Man is would be longer than the one the apostles presented at that time. The more people come in contact with Christ, the more interpretations they give or opinions they form of Him. It is very necessary therefore for those called to ministry in the different traditions and cultures to know the way the different people understand the object of their evangelization—Jesus Christ and His story.

In the brief but effective life of Christ on earth, He had touched the lives of so many people. A great number of the people saw Him from different angles, and therefore, their approach to Him differed accordingly. He was mostly seen as a healer because of the numerous ailments of the people He had taken away. Others saw

Him as a teacher because of His rabbinic methods of presenting His teaching. I'm not sure any of the people knew Him as the Messiah except those to whom His identity had been revealed, like Simeon and Hannah in the temple scene of the presentation when they made some prophetic statements about him even as a baby. Simeon, who, according to the scriptures, was told that he would not die until he had seen the Messiah, held the child in the temple and proclaimed, "Now, Master, you may let your servant go in peace, according your word, for my eyes have seen your salvation, which you prepared in the sight of the peoples, a light for revelation to the Gentiles, and glory for your people Israel" (Luke 2:29–32). For Hannah, Luke writes, "Coming up to them at that very moment, she gave thanks to God, and spoke about the child to all who were looking forward to the redemption of Jerusalem" (Luke 2:38).

So the question that our Lord posed was not just an information-seeking one but a way of telling the apostles that He meant many things to many people and therefore they should know how to deal with it. The apostles themselves were not so sure they really knew their Master very well. If they did, they did not understand Him properly. A lot of what He said was confusing to them. A good example is when the Lord told them to "Beware of the yeast of the Pharisees and of Herod." They totally misunderstood Him and thought it was because they were running low on bread. He took time to explain and then ended up by asking them, "Do you still not understand?" Also in the request of Phillip, "Lord, show us the Father," He responded that to have seen Him is to have seen the Father.

It is apparent that Jesus did not care much about who the others said He was. They were entitled to their opinions. His concern would seem more about who His disciples said He was because, as they were expected to carry on with His ministry, it was imperative that they knew who He truly was. This then made Him to advance a follow-up question, which was very important for the advancement of His ministry: "But who do you say that I am?"

Part 2

But Who Do You
Say I Am?

6

But Who Do You Say That I Am?

Consider a scenario where you have been going with a friend for three years, doing everything together, and people come to regard you as the best of pals and identify you with one another. Just one fateful day, your friend asks you, "Who do you think I am?" Your first reaction would be confusion. Then you find a voice and ask, "What do you mean?" Your friend repeats the question, this time using a different verb. "Who do you say that I am?" There would be streams of thoughts running through your mind. *Could it be possible that I do not truly know who my friend is? Could he be someone more than I take him to be?* In this scenario, one thing is very certain: the friend has presented a puzzle. This would have been the fate of the apostles had Peter not come up with an answer. The Lord Jesus had just asked His apostles what the people said about Him, who people said He was. The apostles confidently responded according to what they had heard people say. Then He directed this question to the apostles as a follow-up.

That He proceeded to ask this question after some answers were proffered to Him, in my opinion, means that those other answers, whoever people outside said He was, did not matter very much to Him at that particular moment. He wanted to know of the apostles' knowledge of Him. He would love to hear their version of the answers. This would very much tell of their relationship with Him. Several years after this question was asked, the answers to it still differ when answered from the human point of view.

It is very obvious that this question is as relevant today as it was in the days of the apostles. It is a perennial question in Christendom. A critical mistake one would make would be to treat this question as if it belongs only to the time of the apostles. This is a question whose answer directs our entire Christian life. To every believing, Christian this question becomes personal and the answer to this question determines where the individual stands. One's definition of Christ expresses the individual's relationship with Christ. In the context of an interpersonal relationship, it's like Christ saying, "Who am I to you?" It is the most important question of our life. The answer to it forms the foundation of our faith.

If Jesus had appeared as a sort of enigma, generating different understandings and opinions of Him in the general public, there was a group that was expected to know who He really was. By virtue of their closeness to Him, as they were members of His inner caucus, they were expected to know Him better than members of the public. He had told them on one occasion, "To you has been given to know the mysteries of the kingdom of God but to others it is in parables" (Matthew 13:11). On some other occasion, He had told them, "I do not call you servants anymore, because the servant does not know his master's business, but I have called you friends for I have made known to you everything I have heard from my Father" (John 15:15). This statement shows how close the Lord Jesus regarded the apostles to be. He knew He was going to hand over the ministry to them. He opened up to them as a friend would to a friend. Disappointing as it may seem, the reality still remains that not even the apostles then could authoritatively say who Jesus was when He directed the question at them. The speeches and actions of their master were equally as amazing and sometimes puzzling to them as they were to the rest of the people—as in the case when they went out to buy food only to come back and see Him sitting and chatting with a Samaritan woman. Jesus Himself knew this pretty well, and He pointed it out to Peter on the night of the last supper when He washed the disciples' feet. "You do not understand now what I am doing, but someday you will" (John 13:7). There were, however, certain things He had expected them to know, while others would have to wait for the coming of the Holy Spirit. When Philip was eager to know the Father and he asked the Master," Show us the Father." The Lord answered Him with a question, which leaves us with the impression that no matter how long somebody has been with Christ, it could be possible He still ends up not truly knowing who Jesus is. "Have I been with you for so long a time and you still do not know me, Philip?" (John 14:9). This could be very disappointing to such a great teacher. Being with them all this time of public ministry, the Master had expected that they should have known Him more than others. This shows us that of the millions of people who profess to be followers of Christ, only very few truly know who He is and what He stands for. This can account for some of the attitudes displayed by some followers of Christ.

In turning to His disciples to ask who they thought He was, He wanted them to expose what they were thinking inside their minds about Him. Their answers, which would portray their understanding of Him, would make a great difference in the ministerial terrain He was bequeathing to them.

His ministry attracted many followers, and it is apparent that so many people followed Him with different intentions. Even to this day, people follow Christ for different reasons. All these people were Christians because they were followers of Christ. They followed him with two different agendas. Thomas á Kempis said, "Many people followed Christ to the breaking of the bread but only very few followed him to the cross."

Breaking of the bread here would mean the material things of this world, which drew them to Christ. Following Him to the cross would mean following through the way of the cross. Some followed Him to the point of their personal material satisfaction. Others followed through the event of their salvation. Some followed the Jesus who could give food—material wealth; others followed Christ for spiritual nourishment, which leads to salvation.

7

Why the Question?

Asking His followers questions was nothing strange for Jesus in His ministry with His disciples. On several occasions, the Lord Jesus had opportunities to question His followers about their motives in looking for Him. In some circumstances, the questions exposed the clear reason why some of His followers flocked to Him. Some He used to teach the people who He was and His mission, and some He used to warn the people about following Him with a wrong motive, which, of course, some of them did. In the Gospel of John, He asked John's disciples, who, on hearing John point Him out as the Lamb of God, left their master to follow Jesus. He turned and saw them following Him and said, "What are you looking for?" (John 1:38). Also in the gospel of Luke, He asked the people, "What do you go into the wilderness to see?"

(Luke 7:24). But this very question was an epoch-making question that not only defined Him but also produced a leader for the apostles and set His agenda rolling; it was after Peter's profession that He opened up about His journey to the cross.

When the Master posed the question, I'm wondering what was in the minds of the apostles. Did they even think of why He was asking this question at that time? Or were they just thinking it was one of those questions of the Master. If the latter, I think they missed the gravity of this mother of all questions. The Master was well aware that most of those following Him did not actually know who He was, even with all the prophecies about Him. He knew that later in the long history of Christianity, many people would misinterpret Him even the more. After many years of Christianity, how many people truly know Jesus? In the present generation, a lot of people are still following the crowd instead of the Christ.

The question obviously has more answers today than it did in the days of Christ because Jesus has so many meanings to so many people today. The way many people view Christ is akin to the legendary six blind folks of Indostan who went to see the elephant in John Godfrey Saxe's poem. Each of them perceived the elephant from the part of the elephant he happened to touch and erroneously thought the elephant was all that he touched.

All of them ended up defining the elephant from the part of the elephant they touched.

So many people interpret Jesus from their own perspectives. Most people today preach the Jesus who told His disciples "give them food to eat" and the Jesus who changed water into wine. For them, He is a miracle worker who can always change their situation in life and make them richer as long as they pay tithe and sow the seed for a breakthrough.

They do not preach the Christ whose "sweat became like drops of blood" in Gethsemane and who at a point said, "Father, if it is possible, take this cup away from me." Many Christians do not identify with this later Jesus. They do not see Christian suffering as something noble. They are ready to run from one church to another in search of solutions to their problems. Sometimes they fall prey to scammers parading as prophets and healers.

The prosperity gospel, which took shape in the forties and fifties, has a theology that is a direct descendant of this; it teaches that wealth is a sign of God's favor while poverty is a curse from God. This teaching seems to set the standard for some contemporary ministry movements.

For some Christians, God is just there to make them rich and comfortable. These are the people who would always want God to do whatever they ask of Him. If He does not do it, they lose faith in Him. So God should be at their beck and call. In their understanding, this would prove that He is a God of miracles. Anything short of that is not Jesus for them. They do not want to associate with the suffering side of the Lord. Here is what Thomas á Kempis says in the *Imitation of Christ* about this tenet in Christianity.

> Jesus has always many who love His heavenly kingdom but few who bear the cross. He has many who desire consolation, but few care for trial. He finds many to share His table, but few to take part in His fasting. All desire to be happy with Him; few wish to suffer anything for Him. Many followed Him to the breaking of bread, but few to the drinking of His chalice of passion. Many revered His miracles; few approached the shame of the cross. Many love Him as long as they encounter no hardship; many praise and bless Him as long as they receive comfort from Him. But if He hides Himself and leaves them for a moment, they fall into either complaints or into deep dejection. Those, on the contrary who love Him for His own sake

> and not for any comfort of their own,
> bless Him in all trial and anguish of heart
> as well as in the bliss of consolation. Even
> if He should never give them consolation,
> yet they would continue to praise Him
> and wish always to give him thanks.[1]

Thomas á Kempis wrote this several years ago, yet it is truer today than even at the time he wrote it.

There are so many evangelical "ministries" today and many people preaching the "message" of Christ. In many cases, these ministries are piloted by mega rich pastors. It is interesting to observe that in some developing countries where there are high rates of poverty, these pastors are flying around in their private jets. The disturbing aspect of this whole thing is that these congregations who are being scammed are peopled mostly by the very poor members of the society who come out in aggressive defense of their "men of God" against inquiring minds. Some of these pastors are opening private universities in the name of the church and yet are charging exorbitant tuitions, which some of the church members cannot even afford. This can only mean that these ministries are money-making ventures. In most of these cases, the pastors and overseers are among the richest folks in the world, as *Forbes*

---

[1] Book 2, Chapter 11.

revealed, especially in the third-world countries. They call on people to "sow a seed for a breakthrough," and the congregation gladly reacts by opening and emptying their wallets. Elementary Christian theology teaches us that the "breakthrough" moment for Christians was at that awful moment when Jesus, in excruciating pain, gave up the ghost. Any person asking the children of God, who have the same right as every other person before God, to bring money for a breakthrough is simply swindling them. Such a person is serving himself not God. Some men of God are really turning their congregations into ATM machines, all in the name of Jesus. Of all the miracles and healings that Jesus performed, not even once did He charge any money, yet these "men of God" require their congregation to purchase items for healing and pay exorbitant fees for their services.

Another reason I think the question was necessary was that after Peter's profession of faith and his subsequent installation as the "key-holder" of the kingdom, some disciples still failed to grasp the mission of Christ. They still had that expectation of a political messiah who was going to give them political independence. This is depicted in the scene on the Mount of Ascension when one of the apostles asked the Master, "Lord, will you at this time restore the kingdom to Israel?" To which He responded, "It is not for you to know time or season that the Father has fixed by His own authority but you shall receive powers when the Holy Spirit has come upon you and you shall be my witnesses in Jerusalem, Judea, and Samaria and to the ends of the earth" (Acts 1:7–8).

One of the puzzling events in the life of Christ was the transfiguration; it was a scene that left the three apostles who were present totally shocked. A voice they had never heard before addressed them from the clouds and introduced Jesus thus: "This is my beloved son with whom I am well pleased; listen to him." If they thought they knew the Master, this once again threw them off-balance. It must have given them some food for thought when Jesus told them after that strange occurrence not to tell anybody what they had seen until after the resurrection. Surely Jesus was a mystery figure in the eyes of humans, including the apostles.

The mystery surrounding the life of the Master started even at infancy when He was presented in the temple. The event that played out left people wondering what sort of child this would be. The parents were sometimes amazed at the turn of events in the life of the child, which left Mary, his mother, pondering these things in her heart. If at that point in time He had asked even His parents that question, "Who do you say that I am?" I'm not sure what they would have given as an answer, given that He kept shocking them with strange statements that always left them stunned. When they found Him in the temple after three days of searching, in the midst of doctors, naturally one would have expected to hear the little boy say He was sorry to the frustrated parents. When Mary asked, "Son, why have you treated us this way? Your Father and I have been anxiously looking for you" (Luke 2:48), the response He gave was puzzling: "Why is it that you were looking for me? Did you not know that I had to be in My Father's house?" When we look at this from the point of view that both parents had a prior knowledge of who was going to be born of them, we can only sympathize with these mere humans who were struggling to understand the ways of the divine. They had to cope since they had to always surrender to the will of God.

Another reason that this question is very relevant is that it questions the motives of some followers of Christ even now. There are several reasons why people follow Jesus, especially in this postmodern time. Following one's personal ambition instead of Jesus makes a lot of people give different meanings to Christianity. Pope Francis pointed out in his homily on May 5, 2014, in the Vatican that "there are those who follow Jesus out of their desire for money and try to take economic advantage of the parish, of the diocese, of their Christian community, of their hospital or college." They follow Jesus for the material wealth they gain from it. These are the kinds of people who would present one face in public and another in their private lives. These are the ones whom Jesus referred to as hypocrites. The question is therefore relevant today because of those I would like to call the dual-persona Christians, whose answers in public would be very contrary to what they privately stand for.

8

The Dual-Persona Christians

"These people honor me with their lips
but their hearts are far from me."
—Matthew 15:8

When Jesus Christ began His ministry He started by calling those He would use to reach out to the world. The call of the Lord to the people who later became His apostles, which has extended to every believer, was a simple statement: "Come follow me." "Follow me" here means "Come with Me every step of the way. Imitate Me, and do what I do. This is the way of the Father." For those who follow Him, therefore, He tells them, "Be holy because your heavenly Father is holy."

The apostles literally went along with Him in his entire journey. They left everything so as to be able to follow Him. This is expected also of new-generation Christians who respond to this call by their baptism, which is the initiation into the family of God.

One cannot follow him only when He turns water into wine or when He multiplies the loaves. Following Him includes following Him to the Garden of Gethsemane and to the cross.

Why is the Christian influence not so much felt in global politics, which controls the economies of nations? Some countries are so rich yet the citizens are so poor because of mismanagement by corrupt politicians. Many of these politicians are Christians. Violence, disrespect for human life, inequality, and race, gender, and class discrimination are still reigning supreme in the global space, even in countries that profess faith in Jesus Christ. Why is it that a very good percentage of the world's population is Christian yet the world has not yet seen the light? The Master had said, "You are the light of the world; a city built on a hilltop cannot be hidden."(Matthew 5:14). Why is the world still acting like those who do not know God? The simple answer in my opinion is that Christians are conformed to the world and instead of them leading the world to the light, the world is rather leading them. That is exactly what St. Paul in his letter to the Romans warns against. He says "do not be conformed to the world" (Romans 12:2). Some Christians unfortunately mortgage their faith for material gains. There are still some people who are living as enemies of the gospel. Most of these are people in positions of authority. They try to pay allegiance to two masters—the sanctuary and the throne. People who allow party or societal ideology instead of the Christian culture to determine their actions should have a rethink. They perform their religious pieties in order to be seen by other people, as Jesus puts it.

The Lord Jesus, admonishing his disciples, said, "No one can serve two masters … you cannot serve both God and wealth" (Matthew 6:24). St. Ignatius of Antioch, expounding more on that, said, "Do not have Christ on your lips and the world in your heart." This is clearly demonstrated in the persona of Judas, who was a member of the college of apostles. At the climax of his greed, he even kissed his divine master in order to identify Him to the abductors, who had paid him for this service. Jesus pointedly asked him, "Why do you betray the son of man with a kiss?" There are still many "Judases" in the family of God today. Some are there for the sole purpose of benefiting themselves and causing havoc in the family of Christ. They serve themselves rather than the Lord and Master of all. It is even difficult to identify them because they are wolves in sheep's clothing. Millions of Christians around the world today are parading double identities.

People of the world have two conflicting answers to one particular question, depending on what they want to accomplish. For a Christian who has God not just on his or her lips but also in his or her heart, his or her "yes" will always be "yes" and his or her "no" will always be "no," knowing, as the Lord Jesus says, that anything outside of that comes from the evil one. They are not those who say "yes" just to deceive their listeners when in reality they mean "no." These people's loyalty is in what will bring them material benefits. As the psalmist says, "Their belly is their god."

Christians are supposed to be followers of Christ, living their lives according to the teachings of their divine Master Jesus Christ. The early Christians were living in communities and had everything in common. That was a model of God's family. The first couple who tried to double-deal, trying to eat their cake and have it too, as some Christians are doing today, had a bitter taste of the power of the Holy Spirit in a Christian community. Ananias and Saphira sold their property like others did, but unlike others, they decided to keep back some part of the proceeds before presenting the rest to the apostles. In their minds, they felt that it was too much to share everything they had with others, and yet they were parading as Christians. They tried to combine two cultures, the worldly culture and the then Christian practice. Peter reprimanded him for lying to the Holy Spirit, and the outcome was tragic, as we read in Acts 5:1–11. That was the typical example of the dual-persona Christians. The Lord Jesus referred to them as worshipping Him with their lips while their hearts were far from Him. You hear a Christian shouting "Hallelujah!" to God on Sunday, but deep in his or her heart, there is a strong animosity for a fellow Christian who is also worshipping in the same church. There is resentment for somebody he or she regards as "the other," who does not belong either in the same class, gender, or race. Some will come out to smile and shake hands with a fellow christian yet get behind to say ill things or plan evil against the person who shares the same cup in the church. The high point of such a Christian is what the psalmist says: "With their mouth they utter blessing but in their heart they curse" (Psalm 62:4).

Christians are not movie actors whose on-screen and off-screen lives are two different things. Christianity is a way of life, and those who profess it live it daily. Contrary to the teachings of the Master, most Christians live this double life where their "church life" is different from their "out of church life." For this group of Christians, the important thing is just to show up at a church gathering and sometimes make their presence felt. Jesus condemned the Pharisees who entered the worship areas with such attitudes. He referred to them as hypocrites and whitened sepulcher. This is really a cancer in the life of the church today.

During his homily on February 16, 2014, Pope Francis addressed this cancer. This is what the Holy Father said: "Therefore not only must one not make an attempt on the life of others, but one must not even pour on him the poison of anger and hit him with slander, nor speak ill of him. And here we arrive at gossip. This is destroying the spiritual health of the members of the body of Christ. Gossip can also kill, because it kills the reputation of the person." Gossip, according the *Oxford Dictionary*, is "casual or unconstrained conversation or reports about other people, typically involving details that are not confirmed as being true." The flock of Christ has sadly fallen so deep into it. This cannot come from the Holy Spirit.

The telephone has provided us the luxury of sitting in the comfort of our homes and discussing for hours without stepping outside. A lot of Christ's faithful spend so much time on the phone talking about fellow Christians in a manner that kills their reputations. We spend more time on the telephone than in prayer.

A lot of Christians are victims of gossip, which affects not only their careers but also their mental stability. The unfortunate thing here is that this gossip is generated by their fellow Christians who live double lives—the dual-persona Christians. A true Christian would not spread unconfirmed stories about others. The concept of fraternal correction would make this person talk to the other person, and one is bound by Christian charity to correct a brother or sister when he or she derails, not just go about spreading the news around. Some people are more interested in what is going on in other people's lives than taking care of their spiritual lives. The interest they have in other people's affairs is not for them to help but to have what to gossip about.

Every Christian had an ugly side before his or her encounter with Jesus. That is why St. Paul admonishes, "You should put away the old self of your former way of life, corrupted through deceitful desires … put on the new self" (Ephesians 4:22–24). That corrupt nature should have been washed away when we accepted Jesus at baptism. To be a Christian and still remain in the garb of the old nature makes one live a double life and think like the people of the world. This double-dealing by some Christians creates the opportunity for the evil one to use this chance to wreak havoc on the flock of Christ.

Some men of God today are exploiting the desperate situations of some of their followers. The people who are disappointed by the secular leaders try to find solace in their spiritual communities only to be duped by those they trust. They are wolves in sheep's clothing, masquerading as prophets, pastors, healers, and evangelists in order to deceive God's faithful. Healing ministries and miracle centers are flooding some parts of the world, especially the third-world countries, to lure the gullible humans into the den of the evil one. They do all these things in the "name of Jesus." A Christian should not exploit the misfortunes of a fellow Christian, selling oil, water and soap to the members of their congregation for the purpose of healing and driving away evil spirits, which they themselves prophesy to be tormenting the members.

A Christian who has Jesus on his or her lips and the world in his or her heart will always see religion as part-time activity or an avenue to enhance his or her financial base. He or she would use the name of Jesus to enrich him- or herself. Commercializing Christ's name has sort of become a business for some people today.

The only occasion in which our Lord was known to have used physical force to chastise people was the scene in the temple where people were selling and exchanging money. He was furious because they were desecrating the divine space—a place of worship. He even cited the Old Testament scripture Isaiah 56:7 to show that what they were doing was wrong. "It is written, 'My house shall be called a house of Prayer' but you are making it a robbers' den" (Matthew 21:13). In today's churches, a lot of pastors turn their sacred spaces into money-making arenas. There are some terminologies that have come into the ministry arena that were unheard of in the early days of Christianity. Some evangelists will urge their congregation today to "sow a seed," meaning the people should bring in money to buy God's favor, regardless of the fact that God's favors are not purchased with money. Others will ask the congregation to sow a seed for a "breakthrough." In the name of Jesus, so much is happening in the church. Others are ready to fight over a generous donor to the church who decides to worship in another church. Fat donors in churches are honored and assigned special places in some churches. These are mostly observed in independent congregations that do not have a structural hierarchy to which they are accountable. The pastor is the sole leader, and he pilots the affairs of the church as it pleases him. Some of them use the gospel of fear to extract money from their congregation.

On November 24, 2014, in the Vatican City, Pope Francis preached a homily on the desecration of the temple, a homily, which even though it was preached to a Catholic audience, was perfect for all Christians. Here is what he said: "When those who manage God's temple and its ministry, including priests and laypeople, become businessmen, people are scandalized. And we are responsible for this. It is scandalous when the temple, the House of God, becomes a place of business." Those who engage in this have a different definition of Jesus. For some postmodern men of God, church is business. According to St Paul, "such people are false apostles, deceitful workers, who masquerade as apostles of Christ" (2 Corinthians 11:13). They parade themselves as the "men of God" when actually they have turned themselves into "gods of men."

If the teachings of Christ were strictly followed, which would mean that everyone truly knows who the Son of Man is, the world would have been a better place than it is today. The Lord Jesus told His disciples, "By this the world will know that you are my own, when you love one another" (John 13:35). To be a true disciple means no discrimination against one another. This is the type of community that Paul describes in his letter to the Christian community in Colossae. "In this new life, it does not matter if you are a Jew or a Gentile, circumcised or uncircumcised, barbaric, uncivilized, slave, or free Christ is all that matters, and he lives in all" (Colossians 3:11). That is what a perfect Christian community should look like. Anyone who continues to harbor discrimination and still professes to belong to the body of Christ is simply operating a dual personality. If a person treats another person differently just because the other is different from him or her either by race, class, or gender, it is likely that the Jesus this person is serving is quite a different one, not the same one who came to die for all. It is true that every Christian lives in the midst of a "wicked and perverse generation," according to St. Paul, but we are supposed to shine as brightly as stars. If we live this double-standard life, there is no way we would be able to shine out and influence the outside world. This, therefore, becomes a disappointment to the Lord, who died for us. He admonished His disciples: "Let your light so shine before men that seeing your good works they may give glory to your father in heaven" (Matthew 5:16).

In the scripture God asks His people to be straight forward and take a stand. Hear what he says: "I know your deeds that you are neither cold nor hot; I wish you were either cold or hot. So because you are lukewarm, and neither hot nor cold, will I spit you out of my mouth" (Revelation 3:15–16).

9

The Question Turns Personal

This question, thrown at the feet of the apostles then, is still very lively today for the individual Christians, which in the contemporary context would make it more of a personal question. Imagine the Lord Jesus now standing before you, calling you by your name and posing this question to you, "but you [Your Name] who do say that I am?" Think about that for a moment and try to give your personal answer to the Lord. The answer I'm sure would be different from what others would give. If you try to give an answer that you read from books or what others have said, you are basically answering the first question: who do people say the Son of Man is? Everybody defines Christ according to his or her relationship with Him. Your answer tells more about you in relation to Jesus than who Jesus is in general. Anais Nin has been credited for having said that "we see things as we are not as they are." What seems to be the tenet in Christianity is that we form our Christ's image according to our whims and caprices. This then attests to the different shades of theological doctrines of Christology, which we have seen in Christianity today.

There are certain situations where a general question is thrown to the public and it makes sense only when approached from a personal perspective. This then puts the respondent in the right frame to give a useful answer. It gives room for a personal reflection and connection with the Lord. The greatest disservice we can do to our spiritual lives would be to look at that question as relating to the apostles alone or, worse still, as one of those stories in the Bible about Jesus Christ and His apostles. In that case, we lose that personal touch and the lesson therein that it conveys, leading us to interrogate our personal relationship with the divine Master. Do I have a personal definition of Christ based on my spiritual union with Him? As Jesus says, "If anyone love me, he will keep my word, and my Father will love him, and we will come to him and make our abode with him" (John 14:23). At the end of the day, this question becomes more personal. How does my knowledge of Christ, which I gain through the teachings of the church and the scripture writings help me to act in situations where I am challenged as a Christian—that is, when my Christian faith is challenged? Is my knowledge of Jesus deep enough to enable me to weather the storms of life? Does my knowledge of Christ help me to see another human being as myself, irrespective of where the person comes from? How about attending to the needs of others? Has my knowledge of Christ and my relationship with Him made me to see Him in my neighbor?

You must have read so many books about Christ aside from the Bible, watched many audiovisual programs, and listened to many sermons on Jesus. Unless you try to answer the Lord from your personal relationship with Him, it becomes a futile endeavor to parade yourself as a Christian because you are simply following the crowd. There is no personal touch; you are just following what others are doing. It is no better than the answers the apostles gave to Christ: "Some say John the Baptist, some Elijah or one of the prophets." But you, who do you say that Christ is? The question calls us to identify with and experience Him in our Christian vocation through personal sacrifice. Simon of Cyrene carried the cross behind him, and Nicodemus surrendered his new tomb for Jesus to be buried in. These were people who really had that personal touch with Him. There were others who did not have the personal touch but gave away something because "the Master is in need of it." For example, the owner of the ass surrendered it for Him to ride into Jerusalem, and the owner of the upper room gave it for the Master to eat the Passover with His disciples.

To properly identify with Him gives us the courage to do the will of God no matter how tedious. This is what will enable us to hear those words of our Lord at the end of time, "Come ye blessed of my Father," which of course is what every believing Christian hopes to hear in the presence of the divine Master on Judgment Day. One has to ask him- or herself, "Who is Jesus for me in the economy of my salvation?"

In the Gospel of St. Mark, Jesus says, "He who has believed and has been baptized shall be saved" (Mark 16:16). This means here that one needs that personal conviction and belief to gain salvation. One cannot believe unless one truly knows the object of one's belief. To personally know Jesus then helps in the salvation of the individual. Two individuals from the same faith tradition can approach the throne of God on Judgment Day, and one sails through but the other is condemned. Jesus has made this clear in the Gospel of St. Matthew. "Then there will be two men in the field; one will be taken and one will be left. Two women will be grinding at the mill, one will be taken and one is left" (Matthew 24:40–41). This is intended to teach us that two people from the same church may have two different notions of Jesus and therefore respond differently to the message of

Christ, which automatically informs their relationship with the people around them. There is a way that leads an individual to know and understand the true Christ. Pope Francis in a homily on Friday, September 26, 2014, in the church of Sancta Barbara, said that if you do not accept the cross, you will not understand Christ. To accept the cross means carrying it along with Him who died on the cross and was resurrected for our redemption.

In contemporary times, we try to fashion Christ in our own image, the type of Christ we would like to have—a Christ we would be comfortable with. Such was what St. Peter was trying to do when he rebuked Christ for predicting His death on the cross. Christ reprimanded him in strong terms. "Get behind me Satan; you are a stumbling block to me; for you are not setting your mind on God's interest, but man's" (Matthew 16:23). To think like God, which is a must for followers of Christ, we must accept the cross. Then and only then can someone proudly identify with Him.

10

You Are the Christ

When one is very certain of something, one can make a positive statement about it without any fear of contradiction. The statement that Peter made before Christ, telling Him, "You are the Christ," was a positive statement, which nobody can contradict. He said it with the conviction of a person who knew what he was talking about. This was a statement of faith and trust in the Savior Jesus Christ, the one who was to come. Did Peter truly know the identity of their Master before this historic question? I cannot tell. One fact remains very certain; this brilliant answer did not just come from Peter. He was inspired, and the Lord Jesus attested to that. In the scriptures, we have seen some individuals who made such inspired statements of affirmation about Christ, including John the Baptist, Simeon, and Sarah.

When Peter gave this matter-of-fact answer, "You are the Christ, son of the Living God" (Matthew 16:16), Jesus recognized immediately the source of such a great profession of faith by Peter and told him, "It is not flesh and blood that has revealed this to you but my heavenly Father." Peter was speaking not just for the apostles but also on behalf of the generations of Christ's followers, a faith that generation after generation will come to share and benefit from. When the Master said, "Upon this rock I will build my church," He was referring to where salvation will be preached to millions of followers. The building of the church will be the fulfilment of the Father's will of establishing His kingdom on earth, a mission He came to fulfill, building a family that will continue in heaven, so as to fulfill His wish of "where I am you also may be too" (John 14:3).

To acknowledge Jesus as the Christ means one has faith in Him. According to St. Paul, "If you confess with your lips that Jesus is Lord, Faith in the heart leads to salvation" (Romans 10:8b–10). This acknowledgment of course comes with a huge responsibility.

When one is committed to Him, one has to be ready to endure trials and tribulations. The Master had already made this clear when He said, "In the world you will suffer tribulation, but take courage, I have overcome the world" (John 16:33). Be ready to face oppositions as Christ did, for He said, "If the world hates you, you know that it hated Me before it hated you" (John 15:18). In the Gospel of Matthew, He says, "You will be hated by all because of my name, but whoever will endure to the end will be saved" (Matthew 10:22). That is the package that accompanies the acknowledgment and acceptance of Him as the Christ. That is the way of Christ, the cross that every believer should be ready to carry.

In just a brief moment after proclaiming Peter the rock, Jesus had to repudiate him with very strong words: "Get behind me Satan" (Matthew 16:23). Why such a sudden about-face? After being proclaimed as the Christ by Peter, the Lord was telling them of the impending suffering He would have to go through in the hands of the elders, which would lead to His death and resurrection without which our redemption would not come. Peter, in the spirit of his office as the newly crowned leader and holder of the keys of heaven, tried to wish it away from the Master. The master told him point-blank that he was Satan—a stumbling block, an obstacle, a hurdle— because he was thinking in the sense of the world, not as God thinks; the world goes for pleasure and avoids pain and suffering. This therefore means that anyone who is not ready to go through the thick and thin of this life is not worthy of that call. Here is what the Lord says, "And he who does not take his cross and follow after me is not worthy of me" (Matthew 10:38). To say "you are the Christ" means therefore that you have accepted Him and His way of life and should be ready to sincerely journey all the way with Him from the table of the last supper to Calvary.

From the table of the last supper to Calvary, there are some noticeable characters that we should look at here.

Judas—He participated in the Last Supper absent-mindedly because his mind was focused on some unfinished business, which he thought would fetch him some money. He was serving two masters. His attention was divided. He is the example of the dual-persona Christian.

Peter—He trusted and loved the Lord. He respected Him as his Master, but his faith waned in the face of threat from unbelievers. He denied the Master he had confidently proclaimed as the Son of the Living God. He paints the picture of a Christian who would not stand up in the face of trials and temptations.

Pilate—He was a great judge by all standards. He knew the right thing to do but did not have the courage to do it because he was afraid of the people. He had the power to set Jesus free, but he was afraid of what the people would say. He feared the people more than God. Unfortunately he did not have the opportunity of hearing what Jesus had said: "Do not fear those who kill the body but are unable to kill the soul; but rather fear Him who is able to destroy both soul and body in hell" (Matthew 10:28). Many Christians in positions of authority find themselves in such situations and like Pilate they fail to do the right thing because they fear the people more than God.

Mary Magdalene—She was faithful and held on to Jesus even after He was dead and buried. She was not afraid of the soldiers stationed to guard the grave in which Jesus was buried. She went out alone even in the dark to anoint the body of Jesus.

The Two Thieves—One recognized Jesus as a king even though he barely knew Him and asked to be remembered when He entered His kingdom. The other was interested in being taken down from the cross probably so that he could go and continue with his life of crime.

Joseph of Arimathea and **Nicodemus**—They buried the Lord Jesus.

Every Christian has these character roles open to him or her. It depends on which character role one wants to play on this journey with Christ to the cross. There is always an end to whichever character anybody plays, either good or bad.

"You are the Christ" is a powerful statement that opens the door to salvation, for to profess Jesus as the

Christ is to tell Him, "I recognize and believe in you as the son of God." This, of course, is what leads to our salvation. The Father's will, as Jesus tells us, is that those who see the Son and believe in Him have eternal life. "For this is the Will of my Father, that everyone who beholds the Son and believes in Him will have eternal life, and I myself will raise him up on the last day" (John 6:40). St. Paul, writing to the Romans, says, "If you confess with your mouth Jesus as the Lord, and believe in your heart, that God raised Him from the dead, you shall be saved" (Romans 10:9).

Once one acknowledges Jesus as the Christ, just like Peter professed, within the context of our Christian vocation, there is an implied follow-up question by the same Lord with which He seems to say, "If you acknowledge me as the Christ, do you love me more than these?" This is a question he asked Peter before He entrusted Him with a huge responsibility of feeding His sheep. "More than these?" in this context would then be those who only offer Him lip service, those who follow Him for their own selfish benefits, or those who follow the crowd instead of Him. If you sincerely answer this in the positive, the next statement from Him would then be, "Follow Me." This is an invitation to a new kind of life, which would make you a light of the world and the salt of the earth.

Some of the people recognized Christ as "Lord" and "teacher," but when it came to the point of commitment, they backed off. The case of the rich young man comes to mind here. He was very interested in inheriting eternal life, but then he was given some conditions to fulfill. "If you wish to be complete, go and sell all your possessions and give to the poor, and you have treasure in heaven. Then come follow me" (Matthew 19:21). How did the young man react to this order? Here is how Matthew presents it: "But when the young man heard this statement, he went away grieving; for he was one who owned much property" (Matthew 19:22). What was he thinking in the first place? He probably wanted to eat his cake and have it too. Did he think he could have it both ways? It looks like it. A sad reflection of this is that this young man is playing a character role that most Christians today fit in. He chose wealth over Christ and the eternal life he was looking for. A lot of Christians are ready to mortgage their souls for wealth, fame, and power. There were mixed reactions among Christians and even Catholics to the pope's continuous call to share the riches of the world with the poor. He is very unpopular among many Christians who see him as being too liberal because of this.

Accepting to follow Him is therefore not just being a Christian but matching your words with your actions by living the life. This is where most people fail as Christians.

For them, Christianity is simply baptism with water and going to church on Sundays and major feast days. One must be ready to let go of certain things to gain the joy of the kingdom of heaven.

Once you accept His call to come follow Him, like the disciples who were called and "left everything and followed him" (Luke 5:11), we are supposed to do the same. To follow Him also means to be like Him in holiness. God told the Israelites, "I am the Lord your God, consecrate yourselves and be holy because I am holy" (Leviticus 11:44). The Lord Jesus repeated this admonition when He said, "Therefore you are to be perfect, as your heavenly Father is perfect" (Matthew 5:48). That, of course, was the major aim of God in creating man. "Let us make man in our own image, after our likeness" (Genesis 1: 26). Being like God is an obligation, not an option. We are called to holiness.

"Follow me" means "Be like me." There is, of course, a follow-up instruction. "Take up my yoke and learn from me, for I am meek and humble of heart" (Matthew 11:29).

By proclaiming, "You are the Christ," and accepting Him as the Lord, you are simply saying, "I submit to your authority; therefore, 'speak Lord, your servant is listening'" (1 Samuel 3:10). This means you are open to His divine message and assignment.

A very important assignment for those who have accepted Him is: "Go into the world and preach the gospel to all creation" (Mark 16:15). In any case, where the individual is in doubt about how he or she would be able to do this, the individual would simply be told, "I am with you always till the end of time." This is a call to evangelize and the assurance that He is with his church and of course the Holy Spirit will give His people power. As He was ascending to the Father, He told His apostles, "You shall receive power when the Holy Spirit has come upon you and you shall be my witnesses" (Acts 1:8).

Knowing Him and confessing Him as the Christ is not just a work of the flesh; it is prompted by some divine assistance—the Grace of God. So a Christian is not just someone who goes to church on Sundays but someone who knows who Jesus truly is and follows Him all the way even when the journey is difficult. He or she demonstrates this by his or her way of life. This can be a sure help in time of difficulties, trials, and temptation. Knowing Him as the Christ helps the Christian to endure suffering as He did and to trust in God the Father as Jesus did, having faith in Him that whatever the Christian is going through will eventually come to an end. This is where the words of Christ to Paul come true: "My Grace is sufficient for you" (2 Corinthians 12:9). To recognize Jesus as the Christ means that when temptations come and difficulties barrage you left, right, and center, you keep standing and always say like Peter, "Lord, to whom shall we go; you have the words of eternal life" (John 6:68).

To proclaim Him as the Christ is to celebrate His resurrection daily in our lives and to be in perpetual thanksgiving to God in our daily lives. Saying you are the Christ means accepting and following His way of life, letting go of the former way of life, and living according to the dictates of the gospel of Christ—a new life. St Paul tells us, "Therefore if anyone is in Christ, he is a new creature; the old things have passed away; behold, new things have come" (2 Corinthians 5:17).

In a culture where one is recognized only by his social status, recognizing Him as the Christ and following Him means rejecting worldly recognition, fame, and honor and picking up the cross for the glory of the kingdom. This would be reflected in the works of the person professing this faith. One cannot do otherwise. St. John says, "Whoever says 'I know him' but does not keep his commandment is a liar and the truth is not in him" (1 John 2:4). How many in our generation claim to know Christ but fail to keep His commandments? He asks us to love one another, but we don't. He asks us to care for the sick and the needy, but we don't. In this case, going to church has become a social routine where people go to meet friends or just show up to fulfill a weekly routine. Once a sermon seems a little longer than they expected, it becomes a problem for them and they become uncomfortable. All they want is a "microwave" liturgy where they jump into the church and jump out. They are ready to spend more hours in the stadium, watching games, or more hours at the beach and don't want to spend an hour in the church. They prefer to spend more time outside than inside the church.

I remember a case some years back where as I was vesting in the sacristy for Mass, and a lady came and asked if I loved golf. I was wondering the reason for such a question at that time, but before I could give the answer, she told me that there was a golf tournament going on at that moment on the television. Her request was that I should hurry over the Mass so that she could go home and watch the game. After presenting her request, she waited for my reaction. I simply smiled at her with no verbal response. I did not want to say something that she might misinterpret. She walked out of the sacristy. How much attention she paid during that Mass is only left to imagination. What I did not understand was why she had to come to Mass in the first place instead of sitting back and enjoying her game. Some Christians go to Sunday Mass to satisfy other people—wives, husbands, children, or pastors. Some would be there just to satisfy a Sunday obligation without any commitment. Such would be there physically, but their minds would be elsewhere. People in this group will always argue about some church teachings that do not favor them. As I told a congregation once, the church is not a grocery store where you prepare your list and go in to shop only for what you want. There are some guiding principles that members are supposed to follow.

The Lord Jesus told his apostles, "I give you a new commandment, love one another as I loved you." He goes further to say, "By this everyone will know that you are my disciples if you love one another" (John 13:35). To proclaim Him as the Christ, one has to keep this major commandment of Christ, which is love. Love is a Christian identity. A true Christian is identified by the way he or she loves. This divine family of God is maintained by this love.

When a Christian professes Jesus as the Christ, the profession of faith comes with challenges, which the Christian must stand up to. This is basically taking up the cross and following Jesus. This will come in different forms. The Lord had already warned His disciples about this when He said, "I have told you these things, so that you may have peace. In the world you will have trouble. But take heart! I have overcome the world" (John 16:33). The road along which a Christian walks is not all that smooth. Jesus, however, called upon us to have faith in Him whom we are following on this journey. There is a cross to bear, but remember there could also be a Simon of Cyrene on the way, waiting to help. Human struggles continue as we go along as Christians. The early Christians went through a lot. Some were killed then, and it is happening now in some parts of the world. Jesus told His first generation of followers, "Strive to enter through the narrow door; for many I tell you will seek to enter and will not be able" (Luke 13:24). This, in my opinion, points to a personally active life on the part of the individual in order to enter into salvation. Though salvation is free, there are some sacrifices expected of us as followers of Christ. There is a "war" to be fought. He recognized the struggle ahead that awaited the Christians, and He addressed His apostles, "And whoever has no sword is to sell his coat and buy one" (Luke 22:36). This does not seem to me like a simple journey or child's play. St. Paul makes allusion to this spiritual struggle when he says, "For the flesh sets its desire against the spirit, and the spirit against the flesh; for these are in opposition to one another, so that you may not do the things that you please" (Galatians 5:17). At the end of his journey, he was able to boast, "I have fought a good fight, I have finished the course, I have kept the faith" (2 Timothy 4:7). St. Paul definitely accepted Jesus, but he also had to fight this good fight to keep the faith in order to receive the crown.

This was also what Jesus meant when He said that if anyone wants to follow Him he should deny himself, take up his cross, and follow Him. That means salvation demands a little bit of our personal action also. We are not just passive recipients of salvation. The early Christian martyrs proclaimed their own "You are the Christ" by the shedding of their blood. In contemporary Christianity, there are similar ways of proclaiming, "You are the Christ." In many parts of the world today, there are so many radical terrorist groups emerging, and in most cases, they target Christians. Many Christians are suffering for their faith because there is so much violence against Christians in the world so many have lost their lives. They are being killed in the name of God. This goes to confirm what Jesus said, "… an hour is coming when everyone who kills you will think that he is offering a service to God" John 16:2. What is expected of Christians is to truly stand up for Christ no matter the circumstance; it is part of the Christian vocation. The response would have to be seen in our words and deeds, which will give God the ultimate glory. "By your endurance you will gain your lives" (Luke 21:19). Being a follower of Christ entails sacrifice. The sons of Zebedee, who wanted an easy way to the seat of honor in heaven, were asked, "Can you drink the cup that I am going to drink?" (Matthew 20:22). The Disciples of Christ reacted to this request by the children of Zebedee.

It was this reaction that Jesus used as an opportunity to teach us about leadership; it is a service not a position of honor. In some church communities, we hear of division caused by power tussles among the followers of Christ. This is because people aspire to positions of leadership in the church for selfish reasons. From what Jesus asked the sons of Zebedee, we can learn that there is always a cup to drink.

Once one proclaims Jesus as the Christ, one should be willing to accept suffering for the sake of Christ. That is the way of showing and confirming that one believes Him to be the Christ. The way we respond to the daily crosses that come our way and the difficulties and the temptations on our journey as Christians bear eloquent testimonies to this profession. This is what will earn the Christian that title on the last day, "good and faithful servant."

Christians are expected to live up to their responsibilities as followers of Christ. Such was the norm in the beginning of Christianity when everybody was everybody's keeper. They deserved the name "brethren" because they truly were. Today the situation has changed, many Christians care more about their own welfare than that of their brothers and sisters. Love of one's neighbor gives birth to good works. These good works are brought about through self-denial, which is what marks out a

Christian. This is the way to glorify God with one's life. This is what Jesus means when He says, "Let your light so shine before men that seeing your good works they may give glory to your father in heaven."

St. John makes us believe that "The way we can be sure that we have knowledge of him is to keep his commandment" (1 John 2:3). To know Him as the Christ means also recognizing Him in your neighbor, for the Lord Jesus had said, "Truly, I tell you, whatever you did for one of the least of these brothers and sisters of mine, you did for me" (Matthew 25:40). The Lord Jesus sees Himself in His people. Anything done for any of His people He sees as rendering to Him. Even in the case of oppressing His faithful, He sees that as oppression on Him. In the Acts of the Apostles, when He confronted Saul on the way to Damascus for arresting and torturing the Christians, He asked him, "Saul, Saul, why are you persecuting me?" (Acts 9:4). To profess to know Him therefore and fail to see Him in the sick, the needy, and the stranger is an absurdity.

During His physical life on earth, Jesus mostly identified with the less-privileged, and if one professes to know Him but ignores the less-privileged or at worst fights against their well-being, such a person is a liar. That person might even be seen as fighting against Christ. As St. John puts it in his writing, "Whoever claims to love

God yet hates his brother or sister is a liar. For whoever does not love their brother and sister, whom they have seen, cannot love God, whom they have not seen" (1 John 4:20). When so many people present themselves as devout Christians but inwardly harbor hatred against those who are not of their class, race, or gender, know that such religiosity is faulty.

Every Christian who accepts the word and subjects him- or herself to baptism is professing with Peter, "You are the Christ." This is the beginning of his or her journey to salvation—a journey with Christ to His death on the cross and resurrection. The Lord Jesus told His disciples: "He who believes and is baptized shall be saved." Believing here is not just following others to the church and bearing the name Christian. It means being a Christian in words and in actions.

This Christian is therefore subject to Christ's instruction: "If you love me keep my commandment." Keeping His commandments is a big issue because anything outside this means the individual is just following the crowd and stands the danger of hearing Christ on the last day saying, "I do not know you." At this juncture, the purported Christian will start saying, "We ate and drank at the table with you." The truth here remains that the person was just doing it for others to see or for his or her own personal gains. Eating and drinking with Him does not necessarily mean that one has a direct connection with Christ. Many Christians receive Communion but are not in communion with the Lord and keep acting like pagans. These are the people of whom the Lord Jesus says, "These people honor me with their lips but their hearts are far away from me." St. Augustine says, "Make sure your life does not contradict your words." St. Ignatius of Antioch says, "Let me not only be called a Christian, but prove to be one."

In this case, they will have no share in the kingdom, for He has already said, "Not all those who call me Lord, Lord will enter the kingdom of heaven but only those who do the will of my Father." There is supposed to be a personal touch with the Lord that one receives in the Eucharist.

To profess to know and love Christ but act contrary to His command amounts to betrayal, and it's hurtful not just to the body of Christ but to Christ Himself. Every person is a treasure to Him, especially those who profess to be His followers. He values them to the point of giving up His life for them. The unity of this body of Christ is very important to Christ.

Anything done either by omission or commission that does not comply with His dictates is always very disappointing to Him. This amounts to betrayal, and any act of betrayal makes Him sorrowful. On the night of the last supper, one of His apostles acted in a way that caused Him deep sorrow. This is clearly depicted in the writing of St. John as he reports what happened on that night. "Reclining at table, Jesus was deeply troubled and testified, 'Amen, Amen I tell you, one of you will betray me" (John 13:21). He said this in reference to Judas, who even though he was one of the apostles, connived with the high priests to sell his master. Anytime we act contrary to His teachings, we are betraying Him and we cause him to be "deeply troubled." It is a clear case of double dealing if one proclaims, "You are the Christ," and then turns around to betray Him by taking actions that are contrary to the teachings of Christ. This is another case of people honoring Him with "their lips" while their hearts are far away. Professing Him as the Christ and following Him means you are ready to lay down your life for Christ if necessity demands.

It would be difficult for one to be prepared to lay down one's life for Christ if one does not trust or believe in Him. Unless one is prepared to "drink the cup" He drank, one cannot truly proclaim Him as the Christ. When the apostles were persecuted and jailed by the ruling authorities of their time, they were not dispirited. They spoke boldly before the authorities and told them "We must obey God rather than men" (Acts 5:29). Many Christians today play Pilate. Instead of standing up for the truth and doing what is right and just, they succumb to pressure from the public. The fear of offending people becomes their guiding principle instead of the universal law of love and justice. "We must obey God rather than men." That is truly taking a stand for Jesus, knowing that He is going to be our supreme judge at the end of time, not humans.

The three young men in the flame of fire as recorded in the Old Testament, Shedrach, Meshack, and Abednego, even before the coming of Christ, knew how to be committed to their faith. They testified by their action that it is better to obey God than men. They were not fortunate to see the days of the Son of Man, but their action made the evil king to see the "Son of God." As the king put it, "Did we not have three men tied and put in the furnace? I see four men loosed and walking about in the midst of the fire without harm and the appearance of the fourth is like a son of the gods" (Daniel 3:24–25). The Son of Man, who, before Abraham ever was, had been, was able to be present with those who were committed to their faith, appearing to a pagan king "like a son of the gods."

The trend in contemporary society is that some politicians are prepared to trade their faith in exchange for votes. They are ready to sell their consciences in utter disregard for their church teachings just to protect their party ideology. After all the manipulations and the people vote for them to become their president, senator, governor, or member of the House of Representatives, they congratulate themselves and feel fulfilled.

Here is something any aspiring politician needs to remember. At the end of the day, you are still a human being. When you go to bed at night, you are just sleeping as an individual subject to the law of nature. When you enter the shower to have a bath, the water is not running on a president or senator or governor but on an individual who was created in the image and likeness of God. That is the person who will stand before God to render account, not President This or That or Senator This or That. At that moment, there is no political party, no member of your constituency; you are just yourself, standing before the supreme judge. Imagine a scenario where you as a one-time very popular politician appear before the supreme judge, and He just looks at you without uttering a word. You stand there confused, not knowing what to do, and the eternal judge keeps looking at you silently. As you were about to open your mouth, even though you are not sure of what to say, an overhead screen suddenly appears behind the throne where the judge is sitting slightly above His head such that you see the screen clearly. Then some writing starts crawling from the bottom part of the screen, scrolling upward, and it reads, "For what does it profit a man to gain the whole world and forfeit his soul?" (Mark 8:36). At that point, there is a flashback of all the issues you fought rigorously to install or kill so that you could gain favor from your party or sponsors. As you watch, the writing fades out and more appear. Then you turn your gaze again on the judge sitting before you, and still His face remains blank and staring at you. The new writing reads, "Who did you think was going to be your judge? And what did you think you were going to be judged on, your party ideology or the law of God?" Then you ask yourself, "Why did I not think of this while I still had the opportunity?" It is a question that a lot of people will find themselves battling with at the end of time.

To proclaim, "You are the Christ," and profess to follow Him yet act contrary to His teachings is weird. It is a betrayal of that vocation. This type of attitude made Mahatma Gandhi say, "I love your Christ but I hate your Christians because your Christians are quite unlike your Christ." For him, Christians do not live up to expectations. He felt that Christians do not truly follow the footsteps of Christ, though I have to say that I disagree with Gandhi for using the actions of some Christians to judge all Christians. He should have given credit to some who are trying to live the life. However, the contradictory lifestyles of some Christians are bad examples that do not allow other people to accept the teachings of Christianity. Some even mock Christianity because of this.

Whenever anybody stands up for the teachings of the church, whose authority comes directly from Christ, even in the face of difficulties, he or she is simply saying, like Peter, "You are the Christ, the Son of the living God." As John in his epistle puts it, "Anyone who acknowledges Jesus as the son of God, God dwells in him" (1 John 4:15).

11

... And They Come to Know

"Yes Lord, I have come to believe that
you are the Christ, the Son of God, the
one who has come into the world."
—John 11:27

In his tweet of April 15, 2014, His Holiness Pope Francis said, "Each time we encounter Jesus, our life changes." Jesus had this charisma and ability to elevate any individual who experienced His divine touch. The four Gospels are replete with Jesus's interactions with the people. One particular feature of these interactions is that no one has ever come in contact with Him faithfully and remained the same.

In the Gospels, most people who came to know Christ did that through personal interactions with Him. Many people, however, saw Him and interacted with Him but did not have full knowledge of Him. Others came to Him because they had heard about Him. All knowledge of Him came through interaction. Of course, it all depended on the level of interaction and their disposition. There was always a point of contact—an epiphany moment that led to full knowledge of Him for all who were able to seize such moments. There must have to be a disposition toward Him that would lead to the divine touch.

Cases abound in the Gospels where people experienced their epiphany when they encountered the Lord. A lot of the disciples believed Him because of His works—miracles.

One of the most important figures in the New Testament who came to know Christ through His contact with Him was Saul, who later became Paul. Ironically, he did not meet with Christ when He was physically walking among them. He had a dramatic encounter on his way to Damascus to arrest Christians. A strange power enveloped him, shining a powerful light into his eyes. During the encounter, he asked, "Who are you, Lord?" using the word *lord* here means he has recognized that whoever is doing this to him is more powerful than he is and something told him that he is dealing with a superior authority. In answer to his question, the Lord introduced Himself to him. "I am Jesus whom you are persecuting"

(Acts 9:5). He never for once thought that by persecuting Christians, he was directly persecuting Jesus, whom they were preaching. Here Jesus identifies Himself with the Christians.

That was his first direct encounter with Christ, whom he did not know, but right at that moment, he knew that he was dealing with a divine power, something bigger than he could possibly imagine. He had to address him as "Lord." He was ready to do whatever the voice told him to do. It was a total self-surrender to a power he had hitherto been fighting against. He was instructed on what to do. He had a new life and publicly spoke about this encounter. He did not just stop at knowing Him; he shared his knowledge with others by preaching Him, whom he had persecuted. He had to know Him the hard way, probably because of his personality. Many others knew Christ from a milder encounter.

A great number of Christ's followers came to define Him after their encounter with Him. A very interesting case is the man born blind who was healed by the Lord as recorded by St. John. This man had just received healing from the man he thought was a prophet. The man was attacked by the Jews because he said Jesus was a prophet for healing him. Here is what John says,

> Jesus heard that they had thrown him out, and when he found him he said "Do you believe in the Son of Man?" "Who is he, sir?" the man asked. "Tell me so that I may believe in him." Jesus said, "you have seen him; in fact, he is the one speaking with you." Then the man said, "Lord, I believe" and he worshipped him. (John 9:35–38)

The blind man here came to believe after he was cured. He initially took him to be a prophet, but after his conversation with Christ, he realized that he was talking with the Messiah they were waiting for—the Son of Man. He suddenly realized that he had become a beneficiary of the prophecy of Isaiah concerning the Messiah: "Then shall the eyes of the blind be opened" (Isaiah 35:5). He then worshipped Him.

A personal encounter with Jesus has a powerful way of converting an individual and also giving the person the extra strength to proclaim Jesus to those who have not seen or heard of him before. This is illustrated in the encounter with the woman at the well, popularly referred to as the Samaritan woman. She came like on other days to fetch water for her personal use, not knowing that she would end up with the water of life. On arrival at the well, she saw this stranger who had the physical features of a Jew. Ordinarily she would have just ignored Him and did her business, but the stranger asked her for a strange favor—a drink. "Give me a drink," Jesus requested of the woman, and in her shock, she responded, "You, a Jew, ask me, a Samaritan, for a drink?" That was how the dialogue began. At that level, there was still a cultural barrier between them.

After a brief period of dialogue with Christ, the woman, whom Jesus had just told everything about herself, finally responded, "Sir, I perceive that you are a prophet" (John 4:19). Her eyes were opened after some dialogue with the person she saw and thought was just an ordinary Jew. For the woman, that was the closest she could tell of Christ because she, like many others, did not have any idea of a God who came in flesh and blood like man. She must have known or heard about prophets. One thing was very certain for her about Christ; He was not just an ordinary Jew, as she had initially thought Him to be. Unusual as it seemed to her, she did not give up on the conversation with this strange man. She wanted to know more about this stranger, not just for herself but to share the knowledge with others who were as ignorant of the Messiah as she was before her providential encounter. At this material moment, she must have totally forgotten their initial identities. "You, a Jew, ask me, a Samaritan."

She was evolving into a new identity now. She would soon belong to the universal family of the new kingdom, where "There is no Jew or Gentile no free man or slave" (Galatians 3:28). The charisma of this "strange Jew" totally moved her as she rather now tasted for more words from Him.

When the woman was touched by the divine presence, she instinctively did what Jesus told Peter, "When thou art converted, strengthen thy brethren" (Luke 22:32). She abandoned her water jar, ran to the village to evangelize— spread the good news—and brought people to Christ. "Come, see a man who told me everything I ever did. Could this be the Messiah?" (John 4:29). She no longer called him "a Jew," as she did at the beginning of the conversation, but "a man." She came so close to knowing who Christ truly is—God. It is only God who knows everything about everybody. The light of revelation was not beamed on her just yet. For her, Christ was still a prophet who told her everything about herself. At the end of the encounter, one lesson is very clear: she had been touched by the divine presence, and she now identified with Christ by preaching Him to the others.

In some cases, people just knew by His actions that He was not just an ordinary person like them. In the Gospel of Matthew, when he calmed the waves, the people were amazed and asked, "What kind of a man is this, that even the winds and the sea obey Him?" (Matthew 8:27). All these were pointers to the uniqueness of the Son of Man, but still many people did not grasp it. His encounter with the people presented great lessons, which many of them saw, and they believed in him, though others were still ignorant of Him.

Nathaniel's encounter with Jesus, which was through the instrumentality of his brother Philip, is another good example of knowledge through encounter. When Philip told him that they had found the one written about in the scriptures from Nazareth, he sarcastically asked if anything good could come from Nazareth. At that moment, he was still dwelling in the world of cultural stereotypes, where people are judged by a framed construct imposed by another. I doubt if his brother was amused by that derogatory remark. He, however, ignored that because he had a higher motive and invited him to meet the Lord, knowing that there was a lot his brother would stand to gain at the end of the day when he eventually met the Lord.

They set out to see Jesus. Whether he followed out of curiosity to know the Messiah or just in order to tell his brother Philip, "I told you so," after the encounter, I can't tell. Whatever made him follow his brother to see this man, it turned out to be good for him, for he was eventually convinced. Here is how John captures the encounter. "When Jesus saw Nathaniel approaching, he said of him. 'Here truly is an Israelite in whom there is no deceit.' 'How do you know me?' Nathaniel asked. Jesus answered, 'I saw you while you were still under the fig tree before Philip called you." This statement of Jesus touched him and sent signals to his senses. Then he declared, "Rabbi, you are the son of God; you are the king of Israel" (John 1:47–49). In his excitement, he even proclaimed further than what his brother told him: "He is the Son of God, the King of Israel." His brother must have smiled, remembering Nathaniel's initial reaction. "Can anything good come from Nazareth?" Poor Nathaniel, I wonder if he ever heard of the saying, "Do not judge a book by its cover."

The demoniacs recognized the divinity of Jesus as soon as they saw him and shouted out, "Go away! What do you want with us, Jesus of Nazareth? Have you come to destroy us? I know who you are—the Holy One of God" (Luke 4:34). The presence of the divine power always torments the evil one. It is rather interesting that the demon could immediately recognize the divinity in Christ but some of His followers could not, even after some signs and wonders had been performed by Him in their presence. It is amazing to hear the evil one quiver in fear before the Lord Jesus, whom he had tried to cajole into worshipping him at the temptation.

At His temptation, he was asking Him to perform some stunts, like jumping from a high pedestal and turning an inanimate object into food to prove He was the Son of God. He wanted to test His power then. Having been defeated by Christ, hear them screaming and asking Him to leave them alone, knowing that His power was too strong for them.

Mary Magdalene, who had been with the Lord for a while, could not recognize Him on that morning of the resurrection. She thought he was a gardener. In response to a question by the Lord, "Woman, why are you weeping, whom are you looking for?" she says, "Sir if you have carried him away, tell me where you have laid him, and I will take him away" (John 20:15). In our search for Jesus, it could be possible that we meet Him without recognizing Him. Why was Mary not able to recognize Christ? Was He dressed differently? Or was it just an illusion on the part of Mary? When the risen Lord called by her name, "Mary," she exclaimed, "Rabboni."

The case of the disciples on the way to Emmaus is also very interesting within this context. They were discussing the risen Lord as they were walking along. A "stranger," whom they did not recognize at first, just like Mary Magdalene, joined them on the journey. He engaged them in a conversation, wanting to know what they were discussing. They must have been struck by the curiosity of this stranger. They answered Him by posing a question, "Are you the only one visiting Jerusalem and unaware of the things which have happened here these days?" In their own judgement, He was nothing but a visitor; otherwise, He would have heard of the most talked about event in the city within the past three days. At this moment, there was still no connection between them and the risen Lord. They proceeded to their house where they would experience their epiphany. In the breaking of the bread, their eyes were opened and they truly knew who the man who was talking with them was. The stranger was now revealed to them as their Master. The person who had been with them for a long time opened up to them in the breaking of the bread. In the case of Mary Magdalene, it was the voice of the Lord calling her that revealed the Master to her. These were the moments when they were able to truly connect with the divine.

Of course, that is what happens when people are just following the crowd and are not really in touch with Christ. One interesting aspect of this story is that these men were chatting with Jesus and He asked them questions and explained the scriptures to them, yet their eyes were still closed. Their eyes were opened only in the breaking of the bread. Today a lot of Christians can boast of reading the Bible from cover to cover, yet they still remain unconnected with Christ. What does this tell us about those who think that scripture alone, without the sacraments, can get us in touch with Christ?

For some of the Jews, it took them the apocalyptic chaos at the moment of Christ's death—the earthquake, the opening of the tombs, the eclipse, the tearing down of the temple veil—for them to believe in Christ as the Son of God. Here is how Matthew presents the events during the death of Christ. "Now the centurion and those who were with him keeping guard over Jesus, when they saw the earthquake and things that were happening, became frightened and said, 'Truly this was the son of God'" (Matthew 27:54). That is what is happening in contemporary times; there are so many "centurions" who only come to know the truth of the scriptures when it is rather too late.

The sick man by the pool of Bethesda that Jesus healed on the Sabbath was on his way with his sleeping mat when the Jewish authorities confronted him and accused him of breaking the Sabbath. In his defense, he told them that the man who had healed him told him to pick up his mat and go. He did not know Christ before the healing. Even after the healing, he just saw him as a healer. His eyes were opened after his follow-up conversation with Christ. St. John writes thus: "They asked him, who is the man who told you 'take it up and walk'?" The man who was healed did not know who it was, for Jesus had slipped away, since there was a crowd there. After this, Jesus found him in the temple and said to him, "'Look, you are well; do not sin anymore, so that nothing worse may happen to you.' The man went and told the Jews that Jesus was the one who made him well" (John 5:12–15). At this second encounter, he recognized the authority as He admonished him. He therefore concluded that it wouldn't have been any other person but Jesus.

After an interaction with Christ, what follows in most cases is the individual professing openly his or her faith in the Lord Jesus by saying, "Yes Lord, I have come to believe that you are the Christ, the son of God, the one who is to come into the world" (John 11:27), as Martha said at the raising of Lazarus.

After many years of professing the Christian faith, we are expected to say to Christ by our actions that we have had the opportunity of encountering Him in many different ways. He touches us in His words in the Scriptures and in the homilies delivered by gospel ministers in the liturgy. We touch Him in the breaking of the bread. We interact with Him in the poor, the needy, the sick, the homeless, and the stranger. On July 23, 2015, Pope Francis tweeted, "The one who helps the sick and needy touches the flesh of Christ, alive and present among us." We have therefore directly come in contact with the Lord. We are expected to change our ways of life. As Pope

Francis tweeted on August 11, 2015, "The encounter with Christ can completely change our lives." This goes to confirm what St. Paul says, "If anyone is in Christ, he is a new creature" (2 Corinthians 5:17). This new creature is therefore the one who will always answer like Peter: "You are the Christ, the Son of the living God."

Printed in the United States
By Bookmasters